The Passionate Zookeeper

Denise Cox Robinson

Acknowledgements

I would like to acknowledge:

My husband Norman for his support and patience as I worked through the loss of my father by writing this book. Norman has always been "at my side" ready to assist and more importantly, ready to listen. I love you more...

My Mother who continually helped me recall the information collected to publish this book as accurately as possible. To me, she is the "best" Mother ever.

My wonderful son, Chris for the person he is and for his expertise with getting the photos scanned clearly and his continued computer support.

My younger sister, Deedra, for her friendship and for helping me recall the wonderful memories we shared growing up.

My friends for their encouragement and support and for their proofreading- Alicia Gaskievicz, Linda Sullivan and Terri Green.

To William E. Lummus, photographer, of Pflugerville, Texas for donating the cover photo and many others appearing throughout this book.

One day a magazine photographer, William Lummus, visited and took pictures of Coxville Zoo's entertaining and photogenic animals. This particular photo was published locally and also appeared in a magazine. It was selected as the cover of this book, because it has always been one of our family's favorites. It brings back fond memories of our small dog that often drank from a water bowl that was filled because a small Simian monkey loved turning on the faucet to give his pal a drink.

William E. Lummus took these pictures when he was just getting started in the photo business. His next step in his career was to attend Art Center School in Los Angeles. He was recalled into the military in 1941 and spent over twenty-five years as a military photographer.

He told me that his career took him all around the globe and that he had many wonderful experiences with his cameras. At the writing of this book in 2007, Mr. Lummus was eighty-eight years of age and as he states "fully retired". However, he has taken up oil painting and is enjoying some well-received, if limited, success with his art endeavors.

The first story I remember my Daddy telling me began....

*"In 1939, I bought a monkey....
And then I decided he needed a wife."*

"My Daddy"

He was a gigantic man, maybe not visually to the average onlooker, but certainly in his daughter's eyes. The lessons he taught others were invaluable. He taught by example. His spirit was gentle and kind and his love for his wife, children and animals was always evident.

When he was nine years old, his parents adopted a little girl who had a heart problem and needed a brother with a lot of patience and compassion. She played a very significant role in his life even though she only lived a few years.

My father, Alvin Cox, was an owner of a private zoo, named Coxville, in Austin, Texas. Many people brought him abandoned young or injured animals from all around the area, knowing he'd care for them. He learned how to treat their medical conditions and what to feed them. In addition, he built their homes (cages) himself so they could be safe and wouldn't be orphans. He made sure they had plenty to eat each and every day of their lives.

This zoo was the only one in the area between San Antonio and Dallas. If Coxville had not existed, many children in the area would never have had the rewarding experience of learning firsthand about all the animals that share the world with us. Bus loads of children from Austin, Georgetown, Round Rock, Pflugerville, Leander, Waco, Temple, and many other public schools came for field trips. The School for the Deaf and Blind also brought their children annually. Families from all around visited not just one time, but many times, for this wonderful experience.

Daddy operated the zoo for over twenty years, only asking that the public make a donation if they could afford it. Later, in 1960, he asked for a quarter as an entrance fee, but I personally saw him open the gate hundreds of times for those who could not afford to pay. He made ends meet somehow even though he was responsible for housing and feeding numerous animals.

Since his educational opportunities were limited, he was mostly self-taught, but was capable of accomplishing most any task he attempted, no matter the difficulty. He learned a lot of his trade and skills from his neighbors and friends. He put what he learned to good use and became quite an artist with concrete in making cages, dens for the lions, water dams, alligator pools, or in decorative rock work projects.

He was a hard worker, and showed up for work, each and every day, often working alongside his wife of fifty-three years, his three daughters, and his mother and father until they became senior citizens well into their nineties. Most often his days consisted of working from noon until four the next morning. His responsibilities were enormous and he seemed to always enjoy his work like a hobby even though it often required working long days in the extreme Texas temperatures to perform dirty and unpleasant jobs.

My dad was perhaps a leader of the times in understanding how essential it is to respect everyone regardless of class, age, sex, or race. He did an amazing job of "reaching people" and left behind wonderful memories for all those whose lives he touched. He had a gift of making others around him feel important and special. Members of the community felt comfortable in his store and came to listen to his "tall tales". Everyone was made to feel welcome and he helped many people get through their lonely moments.

Another of his characteristics was his generosity. Dad enjoyed handing out free candy or bubble gum to every child who ever accompanied his/her parent(s) to his little grocery store or purchased any gasoline from him.

If he felt that anyone in his store was hungry and could not afford to eat, Dad would see that person did not go hungry. He would come up with some sort of excuse about needing to trim off the ends of lunch meat or cheese blocks because it was not looking as fresh as it should. Lots of time, he would just say, "I just got a new brand of tamales or sausage in and I'd like you to try one and tell me what you think!" During the years of the Depression, either he or his parents would prepare a sandwich free for anyone who was hungry and came in to the Coxville Grocery Store.

The animals loved him and he could walk into the cage of a tiger or alligator area with only a broom and water hose for cleaning. I will always remember him telling me about the day he was in the tiger's cage. While Dad was washing and sweeping down the concrete floor, he accidentally slipped and fell. His head hit the concrete floor and he was knocked out completely. When he awoke, he thought he was a "goner"! Tabu the resident tiger was hanging over my dad's face with his mouth open! But, Tabu was no fool, he knew that he could have one last big and tasty human meal or that he could take care of this human who was dedicated to feeding him his daily meals. So Tabu gently washed my Dad's face with his tongue until my Dad felt like he could regain his balance and get back up again. They were always the best of friends!

Dad was featured on television weekly on the "Uncle Jay Show" and he always looked forward to selecting a special animal for the local children to learn about. My sister and I went with him to show off our new baby lion cubs. We were also allowed to take them to school for "Show and Tell". It was an unbelievable experience to grow up with so many animal friends.

On Sunday afternoons, after church, my Dad would come and get as many of his daughters as he could round up to help saddle the gentle ponies for the pony rides. We lifted many a child upon these ponies and walked around the ring with them, Sunday after Sunday, year after year, charging only a quarter for lots of rounds! Because he was proud of us for working alongside him in one of the hobbies that he loved so much, he made sure that every single quarter was added to our allowances.

It's funny when I think back about my childhood. I was never spanked or grounded; I always knew I was loved and I was taught right from wrong. I wanted to make my Dad proud of me and not disappoint him in any way. Sometimes, this became a little stressful. For example, Dad would pull out a large Boa snake and wrap it around my shoulders to show others how brave I was! This took a lot of extra courage on my part that I didn't know I had.

As a child, I learned to appreciate how good I felt when I worked hard. I learned to treat people and animals with kindness. These values are a big part of my life today. I appreciate nature, its beauty and the animals and birds that surround us reminding us of how very lucky we are to be part of this world today! And I snicker and smile as I recall some of the wild and crazy things Dad did that will remain forever memories and a part of my spirit.

Let's start <u>his</u> story from the beginning...
Birth/Farm

The thrashers were laboring with the harvest of the wheat crops on Monday, July 10, 1916 when Alvin Wilson Cox made his arrival into the world in Ponder, Texas, at 6:00 a.m.   He was to be the first and only son born to Manford and Bertha Cox and weighed 8 pounds and 5 ounces.

Alvin was given his middle name Wilson because Woodrow Wilson was the president of the United States.   That same year, Jackie Gleason and Gregory Peck were born; Boston Red Sox won the World Series; Congress submitted the 18th Amendment (Prohibition) to the states and Congress passed the first law to regulate child labor. 1916 was a leap year.

Alvin's parents: Manford and Bertha Cox

Alvin with his Mother, shortly after birth.

The old "Doc" announced to Manford that he and Bertha had a big healthy boy in addition to a good wheat crop.

Alvin enjoying a bath.

Four generations:
Manford Cox, Lettie Cox, Alvin and Grandmother Beard

Most of the residents of Ponder made their livelihood by farming and ranching so it was not unusual that Alvin was born on a farm.   But no one could have predicted how much he would love animals or that animals would become his labor of love.   He grew up with baby calves, goats, horses, pigs, sheep, chickens, dogs, kittens, mules, and geese for playmates. He was destined to enjoy the company of animals his entire lifetime.

Ponder started about 1914 with several tailors, general stores, a livery stable, a restaurant, a Baptist and a Methodist church. Next came two large businesses: the Ponder State Bank and the Ponder Hotel. Ponder did not have a population of eighty-four until the early 1920's.

By the mid-1950's, the town had grown to have two grocery stores, a café, a cotton gin, a grain elevator, two filling stations, a trucking business and one of the county's last remaining blacksmith shops.

Move to Denton

In 1922, Manford and Bertha Cox were looking forward to a different business opportunity for their family. So when Alvin was just six years old this little country boy got to move with his family to the "big" town of Denton, Texas. There he could live closer to school and attend services at Church of Christ on Sundays with his parents. At that time, no one knew that this young boy would live out his beliefs as a man who cared for all of God's creatures....both great and small.

Denton was to be the town that the Coxes called "home" for the next twelve years. They would be leaving a town of less than one hundred residents to move to a town where the population had more than doubled to 2,558 in 1890. Denton was growing primarily because the Texas and Pacific Railway was completed from Sherman to Fort Worth.

Since Denton was a college town, Bertha and Manford Cox decided to invest in a boarding house. The Coxes kept roomers (about twenty girls) who were students at the Girls' Industrial College (now Texas Women's University) and North Texas Normal College (now the University of North Texas). The boarding house was located at 1407 West Oak Street which was within easy walking distance to the campuses.

The Coxes loved the girls and enjoyed providing a home for them and watching them change into mature young ladies with a good education and bright futures. In fact, one of the girls became a movie star later in life.

To help with rent, some of the girls worked by doing chores involved in the boarding house, since only Manford and Bertha Cox ran it and did all the meal preparation too. Of course, there were no dishwashers then except for the girls' extra hands to wash and dry dishes.

Even young Alvin had to work to help the family. Alvin's first job was to light the stoves in the wintertime for the girls, and each girl paid him a nickel a week. With twenty girls....that made twenty nickels for Alvin's spending money, or $1.00. He started each day about 6:30 a.m., and it was very cold when he awoke.

The girls liked Alvin and treated him like a little brother. By the time he had finished lighting the stoves, his feet would be icy cold. Frequently, one of the girls would tell him to crawl in the bed with her to warm his feet. Alvin would be shivering after he made his rounds of all the cold rooms.

Later in life, when Alvin was in his seventies, he would recall this story with a big smile and a mischievous look in his eyes, saying, "I think the first job I ever had was my best because of the good benefits it had!"

He never had another job in his life where women paid him to crawl underneath the covers with them!

Alvin as a young boy.

PETS

The first spring in Denton, Alvin bought a pair of rabbits for Easter. He helped his Dad build a hutch to keep the rabbits safe. They attached screen wire on the bottom of the hutch so that the rabbits could stay clean. Every day, Alvin fed his bunnies' alfalfa, hay, and rabbit food and supplied them with plenty of water.

Before long, they had multiplied and suddenly, there were a total of eight. He sold all the babies for half a dollar each except for one female that was special to him which he insisted on keeping as a pet. Soon, he had a surplus of rabbits which he later sold to help buy food and, occasionally the family would have one for their table as well. Bertha did a good job preparing the rabbit and it looked as

good as white chicken. But soft-hearted Alvin was never able to eat the little pets he had raised. He decided to trade rabbits for other things for the family. One lucky day, he traded for a small Fox Terrier puppy, which he named Penny because of the small brown spot that was the size of a penny on his back. Penny got out of the yard occasionally when someone would accidentally leave the gate open. Alvin offered a five-dollar reward twice for his return and luckily Penny was returned both times.   However, one day Penny had a bad encounter with another dog and was badly injured.   He never did recover and Alvin lost his first best friend.

When Christmas came, Alvin received another dog, an Eskimo Spitz, and named it "Freckles".   That same Christmas, Santa Claus bought Alvin some roller skates; it wasn't long before Freckles would follow Alvin on his skates.   He had the idea to train her to pull him along.   He made a harness and leash "gizmo" that worked well. Apparently Freckles enjoyed these adventures, as she would wait at the back gate and be ready to go again when Alvin came home from school.

Grandma Lettie Cox

Sometimes Freckles would sneak out the gate and walk along the dirt road to Grandma Cox's farm house.   Alvin's grandmother would take a small metal aspirin tin and punch a hole in it to tie a necklace around Freckles' neck so that a message could be placed inside the aspirin tin. (Ernest Moeller from Bayer Company introduced the pocket sized aspirin "cans" or "tins" in 1917.) It didn't take long for Freckles to come running back home to Alvin to deliver personal notes from Grandma.

Alvin had pneumonia when he was about six or seven. This picture shows how thin he was when he recovered.

One winter, Alvin was ill with pneumonia and Freckles had been for a visit at Grandma's. Faithful Freckles returned home, jumped into Alvin's bed and delivered a "get well" wish that Alvin would always remember. The reason that Alvin would remember this particular message was that apparently Freckles had encountered a skunk along the road home. When Freckles ran through the house to get into Alvin's bed, she had left a pungent and nauseating odor along her path throughout the house. Her adventure challenged the Cox family to eradicate this smell from the entire house...much easier said than done!

Another close encounter occurred one day when Alvin and Freckles were making their rounds. A Boston Bulldog grabbed Freckles by the ear and refused to let go. Luckily, the owner came to the rescue and took a lighted match and put the warm tip to the bulldog's nose until he turned Freckles loose.

When the Ice Man made his delivery, Freckles would jump up and try to lick the ice. The deliveryman would kick at her, which made her mad, and then she would nip his heels whenever he tried to come into the yard. Soon, the Ice Man would not make any more deliveries and was replaced with another man.

Freckles loved to go with the family whenever they made a trip to the farm once a week to visit the grandparents and to get fresh chickens, butter, and milk. Once a week, the Cox family would bring the eggs into town and sell them. Often Alvin would lose sight of Freckles on these trips. He quickly learned that if she got out on her own, she would go several miles to visit her farm friends and stay for a few days. Freckles couldn't get enough of the outdoor life.

Bertha Cox raised canaries and had a large aviary in the back yard. Alvin also had a pet goat in the yard. One day the goat climbed up on a shed and accidentally hit the canary cages causing the door to swing open. Canaries came out flying in every direction imaginable. The Cox's didn't think they would ever see them again, but later they received a phone a call from the college saying there were canaries in some of their classrooms disrupting the education process. It was not air-conditioned then and there were no screens on the windows so in they flew. A few returned right away. Surprisingly at sunset, when it became dark, most of them found their way back home and through the open doors back into their cages on their own.

Early Days of Employment

Like a lot of young boys, Alvin enjoyed playing football. One day when he was about nine, he was playing a game with some boys down on the corner. Sitting on the side of their playing field was a funny looking building that belonged to these boys. Alvin asked if it was a soda pop stand. The boys said "yeah, but we don't have the money to open it up." They offered to sell it.

Immediately, Alvin saw an opportunity and asked the selling price. They replied "$5.00." Alvin only had a quarter at the time. Deciding that a quarter was better than nothing, the brothers talked it over and decided that they would sell it to Alvin anyway. Then Alvin asked how he was going to move it down to his house as he lived a half a block away. The boys offered to help, so it was carried by all the team and set down in front of the Cox's boarding house.

Soon after, the next door neighbor came over when he saw this new soda pop stand that was nothing more than a remodeled chicken pen, sitting in front of the house. He didn't like the idea very much, but he did like Alvin, so he didn't interfere. He asked when Alvin was going to open. Alvin said he'd be ready as soon as he could get some soda pop.

Another neighbor was a contractor and suggested that Alvin paint the stand. He offered to give Alvin the paint that he had leftover from painting his office. Alvin worked hard to paint the stand, and then his mother pitched in. Bertha went to town and bought some oilcloth. She "dressed up the stand" by cutting out some scallops to tack around the customer window openings.

Things began to roll right along and it looked like Alvin would soon have his little business up and running. Next the soda pop salesman came by and gave him a sign saying "Coke". Soon another one came by and provided a "Dr. Pepper" sign. Then a soda pop man gave him a cold box to keep the pop in.

Alvin went to the ice house and bought ice for the pop. At last he felt that he was ready for his "Grand Opening"! Alvin's idea paid off and he was soon a successful young entrepreneur! In those days, it didn't take long for news to travel by word of mouth of the neighborhood children plus the boarding house girls. Before he knew it; he had a lively business.

The same year that Alvin turned nine, he had "no idea" how his future was about to change. He could never have anticipated what surprises God had in store for the Cox family in December.

The year ahead would bring his family more joy than any of them could imagine followed by a sadness that would never go away....

The Surprise Blessing

News headlines on the front page of Vol. XXV No. 101 Denton, Texas, Thursday Afternoon, December 10, 1925 newspaper read as follows from the Denton Record Chronicle:

"Over 800 Birds Entered in Annual Poultry Show...

Atrocious Acts of Violence Charged to Turks in Mosul...

Sheriff Gives Man $10 for Shooting Turkey Thief...

Shot Man in Sanitarium...

Two cases of Scarlet Fever North of Town...

$11,000,000 Loss from Early Freeze in Northwest Texas..."

Some in Compulsory Law Age Not in School, Doggett Says...

Man Given Year on Dry Law Conviction...

U.S. May Be Past Peak of Production in Some Minerals...

Weather Conditions Keep Down Rail Operating Costs...

As startling as these headlines read, what leapt off the page for the Coxes was the following:

"Baby Found in Manger North Of Denton still is Unclaimed"

"The baby girl found in a hay manger on the F. N. Riney place north of Denton Wednesday morning still was "parentless" Thursday morning, according to a report made by Sheriff Fry. He said several persons had notified him that they had seen cars stopping near the place on the night the baby was left in the Riney's barn. He said he had found no clue as to who deserted the child thus far."

Lying in a Manger

It was a very cold December day in 1925 when a farm family, the Rineys, with nine boys and a girl contacted Bertha and Manford Cox. The Rineys and Coxes were close then as their children were playmates. When they went to the barn to milk and feed the cows, the Rineys heard a strange noise. At first they thought it was a kitten, but to their surprise, they discovered a tiny, newborn baby girl lying in the hay under the feeding troughs.

This Riney family could not take this baby to nurture as they already had a large family with lots of needs so they took the child to a doctor at the hospital. There the doctor discovered that this little girl had a bad heart. Her valve was leaking and the prognosis did not indicate that this infant had much of a chance for survival.

Upon hearing about this abandoned baby, the Coxes asked if they could adopt her and hoped they could sustain her life through their love and tender care even though they knew she had medical problems. Even though someone else had discarded this baby, the Coxes never hesitated to take her and considered her to be a blessing. They named the beautiful blue-eyed, blonde baby girl "Mary Ruth".

Mary Ruth

Alvin treasured his little sister and carried her "piggyback" just about everywhere she wanted to go. If she walked even a short distance, she would be out of breath and turn blue.

Manford and Mary Ruth Cox

Manford Cox's Employment

Along with running the boarding house, Alvin's father, Manford Cox supplemented his income by selling Watkins products as money was pretty tight.   He sold Watkins from 1924 until the early 1930's from a horse drawn wagon.   He was selling Watkins Vanilla Extract in 1928 when it earned the Gold Medal Honor at the Paris World Exposition.   In fact, the use of vanilla as a fragrance began when young girls who were forbidden to wear perfume, so they sneaked a drop or two of vanilla extract to place behind their ears.   He also sold a lot of Watkins Liniment which was the first product that J. R. Watkins started with in 1868 (famous for relieving one's rheumatic aches and pains).

During the depression, most of Manford's customers were short on cash and wanted to use credit or trade him for eggs, chickens, ducks, or whatever the farmers could manage to part with. Manford left his products on good faith asking that his customers pay later, but he ended up with a big debt that his customers could not pay because times were really hard.

The Teenage Years

Times continued to be hard for many families, including the Cox family, and Alvin's income was needed to help support this family even more now that they had Mary Ruth to support.   Alvin never hesitated to help his Dad, Manford, earn a living and would fill in with many part time ventures such as working a paper route. He delivered papers in the winter and ran a cold drink stand in the summer.   One day while delivering papers, Alvin found another hamburger/soda pop stand that was larger and in much better condition.   After checking it over, he decided to expand his business venture.   Now he was on his way for sure.

Soda pop sold well in this college town, so for several years until he moved to Austin, Alvin ran his stand primarily in the summer because he was in school the rest of the time.

Alvin W. Cox, 14-15 years old

Along with soda pop sales, Alvin could now increase his business with hamburgers, ice cream, ham sandwiches, gum, and candy. He enjoyed cooking the hamburgers and piling them high with everything he could add for just a nickel a burger. Can you imagine a nickel hamburger that tasted good? Business was good.

Alvin's cousin, Margie Lynn, came to live with the Cox family when she was about six years old. Her mother and father had recently divorced. During that time, Margie's mother, Grace lived in California and wasn't able to take care of her.

Margie became a good companion and playmate for Mary Ruth, Alvin's little sister. They were quite a pair, but they could become quite mischievous and could be described as "full of prunes".

Margie Lynn and Mary Ruth playing and planning!

Alvin liked to tell the story about how the girls would go to his soda pop stand and slip out one stick of gum from the packages. Of course, like all children, they liked ice cream so they tested the ice cream by scooping out a spoonful of each flavor and then they took their hands and molded it smooth. They didn't want Alvin to know they had sampled it!

Relocation to Austin, Texas

The Cox's felt that they needed to make a change to support their family in the 1930's, and they wanted to seek better medical care for Mary Ruth. When they looked into leasing the boarding house, they realized they could supplement their monthly income with $100 for other expenses.

They decided to leave the boarding house business in Denton and move to Austin, but not before studying more about the new area they would soon call home. They learned that Austin was named for Stephen F. Austin because he came with the first Anglo colonists in 1821. They knew that their neighbors would be comprised of a variety of immigrant groups of primarily Germans, Swedes, Mexicans and African-Americans. They fell in love with Austin's rolling hills and quickly saw new working opportunities for having their own business.

Manford Cox was offered an opportunity to begin work in Austin. He began advertising for the Governor's election by displaying signs for Ma Ferguson on his automobile. Then shortly after in 1932, Miriam M. A. (Ma) Ferguson the first woman Governor of Texas, appointed Manford Cox as Livestock Commissioner. His job was to monitor the farmers to see that they dipped their cattle for parasites (ticks).

The start in Austin was a rough one and certainly not without sacrifices. This was during the depression and money and jobs were hard to get.

The family paid $50 a month for rent in Austin and Alvin walked several miles to and from work as a mechanic's helper because he didn't have any transportation at the time.

This move did not slow Alvin's ambition or talent to make a dollar! From the time he was six in the rooming house, (his first nickel job) through ninth grade, he invented ways to make money. So in Austin, his first job was as a mechanic's helper at Riegers' Garage. He planned to take advantage of every learning opportunity he could.

One of Alvin's favorite stories occurred when they moved to Austin and had just arrived. The Cox family was living on a river. One day Alvin came upon some Poke Salad growing and knowing how much his mother liked it, he didn't hesitate to pick it for her. He knew that after she cooked it, that it would be tender and delicious to eat. Several weeks later he decided it was time for some more Poke Salad so he went to the river to pick it again. This time, however, he noticed the plant had lots of blooms and that the neighbor had some flowers in her yard that looked just like the plants he had just picked. After dinner that night, he just happened to remark about the coincidence. When he asked what kind of flowers were in the neighbor's yard, he was told "four o' clocks". Fortunately no one in the family got sick so at least they knew they weren't poison because everyone was still breathing after the meal!

The term Poke Salad should have actually been Poke Sallet since this English word actually means greens that are cooked before eating such as collards whereas greens that are eaten raw like lettuce are referred to as "salad".

It seems that Bertha Cox really knew what she was doing when she cooked the greens properly to prevent upset stomachs as these greens are actually poisonous to mammals but not to birds.

Poke Salad is a delicacy in the Deep South that grows in a lot of back yards! Individuals that enjoy it pick the leaves and then put them in a poke which is a paper sack for non-Southerners.

One of the favorite ways to prepare these greens is to boil it, rinse it, and then place the leaves in a large cast iron skillet with bacon drippings and green onions. Some cooks will add scrambled eggs to this dish.

Little did Alvin know at the time that there would be a song written by Tony Joe White called "Poke Salad Annie" or "Polk Salad Annie" in 1969 which would be recorded about the lifestyle of a generic Southern girl. Elvis Presley would make this song famous in 1970. The words went like this:

"Down in Louisiana where the alligators grow so mean

There lived a little girl that I swear to the world

Made the alligators look tame

Poke Salad Annie, Poke Salad Annie

Everybody said it was a shame cause her mama was working on the chain-gang

(A mean, vicious woman)

Everyday 'fore supper time, she'd go down by the truck patch

And pick her a mess o' polk salad and carry it home in a tote sack

Her daddy was lazy and no count, claimed he had a bad back

All her brothers were fit for was stealin' watermelons out of my truck patch

Poke Salad Annie, the gators got your granny

Everybody said it was a shame cause her mama was a working' on the chain-gang

(Sock a little polk sald to me, you know I need a mess of it)"

There is even a Poke Salad Festival in Louisiana.

But that's enough about Poke Salad; let's get back to the real story about the move to Austin and how Alvin goes from a mechanic's helper to a passionate zookeeper!

When Alvin was in his late teens, he had finally saved ten dollars. One day when he was driving around with his folks, he saw a service station that had closed up. He wondered if the owners would rent it and copied down the address.

Alvin had always been somewhat of an entrepreneur and displayed creative talents at an early age. He liked to bargain and was quite good at it. He and the owner agreed upon $10 a month for rent. But Alvin convinced the owner to let him use the rent money for the first month to fix the windows and paint the building before actually paying rent the following month.

It wasn't long after that when Alvin decided he wanted to buy the place. At first the building was priced at $500 but by then, the owner had gone up to $2,500. This turned out to be blessing, though, as there was a better opportunity ahead.

The move to Austin turned out to be a good one with new business opportunities but relocation would not be the answer for all of the Cox's difficulties.

The sky filled with dark clouds and it seemed that the very worst kind of a storm was targeting the Cox family. Alvin was about to feel an emptiness he had never felt before or imagined.

Mary Ruth and Butterfly

Despite her spunk and attempts to live a normal life, his little sister, Mary Ruth, had a heart condition that was deteriorating and she was losing life's battle. She had spent the last two years of her life in and out of the hospital. On top of everything else, she had picked up chicken pox while she was in the hospital. She would spend six of eight weeks in the hospital, travel home for awhile and then have to return to the hospital again.

Mary Ruth died in October of 1937, leaving a big void in the family and an empty spot on Alvin's shoulders. Alvin's favorite companion had entered and exited his life in unusual ways and left him feeling alone and helpless. Her adopted family had given her their hearts and treated her like a little princess during her short years with them. Her practical jokes and laughter would be forever missed.

The newspaper in Austin read: *"A tragic ending was written in Travis County of the story of a little eleven year old girl who early in the morning of December 9, 1925 was found in a manger on the F. N. Riney farm, 2 miles northwest of Denton. Parentless, Riney found the newborn as he went into the barn to feed his livestock. Two days later, still unclaimed, Mr. and Mrs. Manford J. Cox adopted her. When she was nine years old (1934), they moved to Austin and settled near Walnut Creek hoping to benefit her health as she had a severe heart problem. She was buried in Austin Memorial Park."*

With a letter sent to the Recorder-Chronicle Denton, the grieving family sent a snapshot of the laughing, child with blonde hair at play and asked for it to be published in the paper, thinking that maybe her "birth" mother would like to know where she was laid to rest. It was titled **"Denton's Mystery Child is Dead".**

Mary Ruth had found joy in the hobby of collecting unusual rocks during her limited childhood years. Many friends would bring her rocks and her collection included rocks from every state in the United States as well as many overseas countries. Even if they were not coming back to the area, they would still ship or send small ones to her from overseas. She received petrified wood and the Coxes bought and traded for more to add to her collection.

It was a great loss when the Cox family lost their only daughter. Since Mary Ruth loved to collect rocks, the Coxes decided to keep her joyous spirit alive in a special way. In her memory, Bertha and Alvin Cox started "The Garden" project working many hours a day on this dream and hobby trying to fill the void that losing Mary Ruth had created. Since Bertha was very artistic, she was able to create an unusual rock garden. She could mix her own cement like a seasoned craftsman.

Everyone's favorite part of "The Garden" would be the miniature city, which included this little house, and a tall rock mountain with an electric train that ran around the villages and over rivers. The project included cars, buses, road signs, and highways. Other buildings included a church and a school. Mary Ruth's short life had resulted in what would become part of the Coxes life dream; a special place to enjoy nature.

Bertha came up with the idea of using a lot of Mary Ruth's miniature doll furniture and toys to furnish a little rock home in her memory. It was the kind of "doll house" that Mary Ruth would have been overjoyed to see finished. The detail was amazing and would be a favorite for everyone who was fortunate enough to share the experience of seeing this unusual rock house. The little house even had a rug and ceramic pets on the front steps.

There was even a rock that depicted an old woman on a hill. Included was an Indian Campfire scene along with fossils, flowering shrubs, a large rose garden, and trees that surrounded "The Garden." My grandmother, Bertha Cox definitely had a unique talent and a vivid imagination.

For a few years, there was a Curio Shop with rocks and cactus that Mary Ruth had collected. There was an area with rocks that resembled goats, "The Three Bears", dogs, and other animals such as a cat, turtle, lion, parrot, etc.

There was never any charge to walk through "The Garden", as our family wanted to share Mary Ruth with all the children. However, this container was available for visitors to donate their pocket change. An interesting coincidence is that the donation jug was started on December 7, 1941, which ironically became Pearl Harbor Day. The Coxes planned to empty it a year later on December 7, 1942.

Visitors were offered the freedom to simply stroll the trails among the petrified wood and interesting rock collection.

Bertha and Alvin Cox were dedicated to the continuance of the "The Garden" which would later be named Coxville Rock Garden. The rock garden would become an unusual tourist attraction in the area which would help make Coxville a recreational site offering plenty of activities for the whole family.

The land that "The Garden" was built on was acquired when Alvin only made $750. Instead of paying the outrageous amount to the owner of the first service station at the previous location, he bought fifty-six acres of land covered with native pecan, cedar, elm, bois d' arc, sweet gum, chinaberry and a variety of oak trees just north of the old place and built a service station on it. This location would be about ten miles out north from the city limits of Austin.

Second Cox Service Station

The name of "Cox" was on the old station, and the same name was on the new station. Everything was getting mixed up...thus; it became necessary to change the name of the business.

One day an African-American gentlemen came in the store and he said, "Huh, looks to me like you're starting a town over here as I see you're getting a motel along with your other business." Alvin confirmed the man's observation. The customer suggested that Alvin name the place "Coxville" because down the road south of there was a little town called "Fisksville", and another little town close by named ""Jollyville and another named "Pflugerville". He thought that "Coxville" would be a good name for Alvin's station. Alvin had his reservations about how this new venture would catch on but after the gentleman left, he thought about the name and decided that it was a good idea. He went in the backyard and found a board and a stub (wooden or metal stake) and took a black crayon and wrote "Coxville" on it and then drove it down into the ground in front of the station.

The trees on the property would play a "key" part in building Coxville over the next thirty years. For example, the Osage-orange tree is also called a bois d'arc, or "horse apple" (bearing fruit that looks like monkey brains). The fruit is the size of a small grapefruit and lime green in color and has a pleasant citrus-type fragrance. It resembles the inside of an avocado but has small seeds. While it can be poisonous to some animals, the squirrels like to eat the interior after they chew through the tough skin. Alvin would soon learn that the wood made great fence posts to use around his oat fields. The cedar, oak, and elm trees gave him plenty of fence posts for the horse, deer, goat, and llama pens he would continually need as his business ventures expanded over the years. In later years, when Alvin sold sausage to his customers in the store, he would utilize the mesquite to give his meat a unique flavor.

As time passed, the original Coxville sign was replaced with an electric sign. There was an addition too, as other services were added to include: "COXVILLE SERVICE STATION AND GROCERY".

So Where's Coxville?

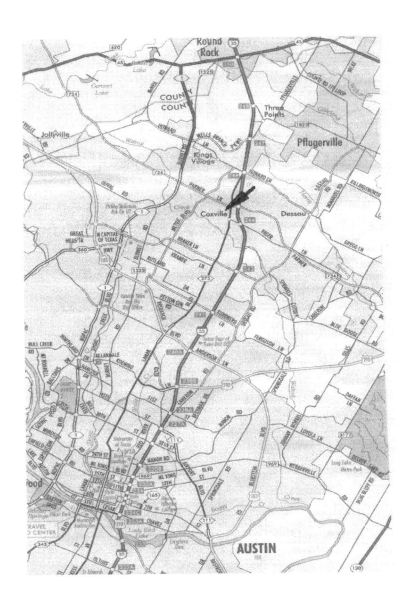

Coxville had a small grocery store complete with mesquite smoked sausage, fresh tamales, lunch meat, Longhorn cheese, chips, bread, soda pop, ice cream, candy and other small grocery items.

Manford and Bertha Cox in Coxville's Grocery

Alvin Wilson Cox

As the Cox's were dealing with their grief and trying to move on, something unexpected happened...something good! They had lost one very special family member, but were about to gain another...someone who would become a key part of their lives, their adventures, and of course, Coxville!

This new person would become Alvin's wife.

And the next part of this story is best told by Doris Cox as she explains how she met Alvin, fell in love, and joined the Cox family. She starts by telling us about their lives in the spring of 1937 and calls this part of the story...

Apples for the Teacher?
AS TOLD BY DORIS COX

I graduated from high school in Fentress, Texas in the spring. I worked nights from 6 p.m. to 6 a.m. at the Telephone Company in Martindale, Texas during the summer of 1937. At that time, the phone company was located upstairs in a building over a hardware store. Then in the fall, I went to SWTTC in San Marcos to major in Business Administration and get my teachers' certificate.

My first date was not exactly a "blind date". Alvin was dating Mary Lois Farrell, a girlfriend from Denton he knew before he moved to Austin. We were both staying at "Mrs. King's" as she had a rooming house and kept twelve girls.

My wardrobe was pretty sparse and consisted of only two or three dresses. No one wore blue jeans to school, but some of the wealthier girls wore nice slacks. I remember how badly my feet hurt from walking several blocks uphill from the rooming house to my college classes in black high heel shoes that had cost me $12.00 from J. C. Penney's. I couldn't afford to buy another pair of shoes.

Alvin came to see Mary one night by surprise, but she already had another date. He was quite persistent and convinced her to arrange a date for him since he had driven from Austin planning to date her. Mary asked several girls to go out with Alvin but they all declined because they were all very busy cramming for exams. I finally relented and thought if he wouldn't keep me out too late, I would go. Mary asked one condition of me though and that was that I wouldn't let him "kiss me goodnight". All went well; he was quite a gentleman in comparison to some of the college students I had dated. We went to the movies and I thought that was the only time I would see him. He dated Mary several more times, but about three weeks later; he called me for a second date. On his third date, he asked to "kiss me goodnight" and then said "That tastes like more!" That was the beginning of our courtship.

On one visit in May when roses were in full bloom, his Mother told him he could cut some roses for me from her rose garden. He cut **all** the pretty blooms off from about 50 rose bushes! He brought them to me in a huge cardboard box. I divided the beautiful roses among the twelve girls in the rooming house. We had roses of all colors in vases, bowls, and any other containers we could find that would hold them.

35

In the summer of 1939, I had my tonsils removed and was at home on the farm with my parents. When he came to visit me he brought me flowers and a box of a dozen-silk stockings. That's when hosiery was made of silk and more expensive and luxurious than those of today.

The second year of my college, I was again studying for exams. My roommate, Azalea and I prepared our own meals, mostly pinto beans and potatoes. On special occasions when my Mother could spare some extras, she would send us eggs and a chicken which was a real treat! One of my close friends in San Marcos worked at a drug store. Alvin knew this and went to see her. He made arrangements to have one pint of ice cream delivered to me at my rooming house. The deliveries were made every night that week.

Alvin or Douglas Fairbanks?

There were several people who thought that Alvin resembled the movie star Douglas Fairbanks (who married Joan Crawford). Whether he did or not is certainly a personal opinion, but Alvin was quite handsome with his bluish-gray eyes, dark ash blonde hair, and tanned face. He was of medium build and stood about 5' 10" tall.

It seems that Alvin never met a stranger and had a very easygoing and gentle nature. Later in life, he would develop a lot of laugh lines on his face because he was most normally smiling.

The first flowers he sent me from a florist were salmon gladiolas and that is still my favorite color. He sent me a big box of chocolate candy; not knowing that I didn't like chocolate so all of my friends got to enjoy it for me.

When I was teaching school, instead of bringing "an apple to the teacher", he brought a bushel. I was teaching first and second grade in a small country school; the Latin School in Staples, Texas which was just for Spanish-Americans. (Staples, a very small town is located about sixteen miles from San Marcos.) Schools were segregated then. I taught in a two room schoolhouse where six grades were taught. At that time students were not allowed to speak Spanish in class or on the playground. My class consisted of about twenty children who were first and second graders. Needless to say, those little ones really enjoyed the apples.

When I see the modern schools today and hear teachers complain about salaries, I remember my first year when I received a salary of $90.00 a month. Later, when I taught in a school for Anglo children, I earned $125.00 a month. I even bought paper and pencil supplies for the children from my salary as this was during the Depression and many of the children were unable to purchase the supplies they needed for school.

For my birthday in 1940, my sweetheart bought me a squirrel fur. He worked long hours because he wanted to give me nice gifts. That same year in 1940, he took me shopping for an engagement ring. I selected one I thought was pretty, but he saw one he liked better, a blue-white diamond. I treasured it knowing he had to work extra hours to pay for this special ring. He continued to make payments until after we married.

I was home that summer of 1941. I had been working in West Columbia, Texas as a bookkeeper for Kotzebue's Drug while living with my sister, Charlotte and her husband, Cecil. My younger sister, Josephine, was already working there. When I got an offer to teach that fall in the elementary school in Staples, Alvin came after me. Before school started, he showed up with a wedding ring on August 20th, asking me to marry him in San Antonio that evening. No way could I change his mind as he had already had the marriage license and the wedding announcement was to be published in the Austin paper on August 21st!

We went to our friends there, Eunice and Doug Scrutchin, and they contacted their Methodist minister and we were married about 6:00 p.m. in their church. Their two young boys decorated our car "Just Married". We didn't know it was decorated at first, but drove up to a hotel and the attendant said, "Just Married?" We wondered how he knew.

I've often thought how worried my Mother and Dad were that we didn't come home that night. They thought we had car trouble. After finally informing my parents, we drove to Austin to tell his parents and they welcomed us with open arms. I didn't tell my girls until after we retired that we had eloped.

When we were first married, I was still teaching in Staples. At that time, my class consisted of third, fourth and fifth graders. I stayed with Grandmother Vaughan (my Mother's mother) during the week and commuted sixty miles each way on the weekends to see Alvin. It didn't take long for us to make a mutual decision for me to quit teaching to help with the purchasing and bookkeeping duties in his business. I kept the same business hours as Alvin for the first four years of our marriage until our first baby was born.

Only a few months after I had become Alvin's partner at the store, a young man drove in for gas. Alvin returned inside after filling the customer's tank and I noticed that this man was following very closely behind him. The man pulled "something that looked like a gun" out of his pocket and held it behind Alvin's back.

Unknown to this man, I was sitting behind the counter. Even though I only weighed about 98 pounds, I picked up a baseball bat and hit him with all my strength. The customer stumbled outside the door and fell on the driveway. We held him and called the sheriff. He stated that he didn't mean to harm anyone and that it was only a toy gun. His intention had only been to steal some money. He was a student and also the son of a prominent man. Needless to say, he never had any charges filed against him.

As we were getting settled in our efficiency cabin, things were going well, but the threat of war was always in our thoughts. December 7, 1941, is a day so vivid to me when the Japanese attacked Pearl Harbor. Every family with young men was most certain to be called into service.

My new husband was called up and sent for a physical in San Antonio. He promised me that if he was not called, we would go on our delayed honeymoon. He didn't get called and was sent home. There were three reasons why he was rejected: his feet were flat, he had lower false teeth, and scars on his lungs. He then had to have more tests since they thought he had pneumonia. The final tests showed there were scars on his lungs caused from pneumonia he had when he was in grade school attending the first and second grades. I learned that he had pneumonia three times and almost lost his life. He had been very thin during these years and had fragile health for several years. The iron medicine the physician prescribed for him made his teeth deteriorate rapidly. Alvin's parents took him to the dentist on numerous visits, but the fillings wouldn't hold. The concerned dentist suggested that the Cox's sue the physician that treated Alvin for pneumonia. But the physician said, "That's all I had to treat him with, and it was either give him the medicine or let him die. So when Alvin was only eighteen years old, he already had false teeth in his lower jaw. About three years after we married, his upper teeth were also replaced with false teeth.

Even with gas rationing, Alvin fulfilled his honeymoon promise with a trip to Mexico in 1942. We bought a new Dodge coupe, and as well as I can remember, it cost less than $1,100. We drove to Mexico City, stopping in the valley to get our first meal in Mexico. We were famished and ordered what we thought was chicken, but the bones were dark, so we later thought it might have been a road runner or another more plentiful wild bird. We ate it and picked off what little meat there was off those bones. In Mexico, Alvin took some auto parts to a Mexican Consulate and they treated us like royalty. We went to the Shrine of Guadalupe and other sightseeing places. I still remember the great tour guide because he spoke such good English and had a pleasant personality.

We returned to Austin to begin our lives together with several Pekinese dogs and a monkey named Junior. I knew that my husband loved animals, and that he would like to have lots of pets, but there was no indication to me that he would spend his life working as a zookeeper. Looking back now, I'm not even sure that he knew that he could in fact realize his dream and hobby, and at the same time work daily alongside his parents and raise three daughters.

This next part of the story needs to be told by Alvin. He loved to talk about how the zoo grew and how....

One Pet Monkey Leads to Another

"In 1939, I bought a monkey......
and then I decided he needed a wife."

Photo by William E. Lummus

"Junior", a small white-faced monkey that weighed about five pounds, was notorious about going through pockets and finding peanuts, car keys or other exciting things.

I bought a monkey over the telephone for $25.00 and named him Junior. I quickly found out that there is nothing quite like a monkey to amuse the young and the young at heart. It didn't take long for people to crowd around so they could watch the monkey's antics and tricks.

As newlyweds, we lived in one of the efficiency cottages and worked side-by-side until we decided to have our first baby. Our first little girl, Darlene, was born July 25, 1945.

After Darlene joined us, we found it necessary to add a bath, small living area, and kitchen to the one room house that had been our starting home.

One of Darlene's first playmates would be a pet named.....

Christine

Darlene's first pet was a monkey with the charming name of Christine Churchill. Christine made the local headlines in April, 1950 when she was involved in a $10,000 damage lawsuit.

There is an expression "it takes all kinds" and this pretty well described the customers that visited Coxville. One visitor, a woman with an infected hand from a burn, decided that she could probably make some easy money by stating that little meek and most lady-like Christine had bitten her when she tried to feed her.

After some investigation, a man told of a shady deal or two that this particular woman and her husband had attempted in real estate to make some fast money. We never heard any more from this after the attorney disclosed what was already known of her character.

By this time, Coxville had acquired even more monkeys so Christine had other friends that supported her in times of trouble. African Green, Rhesus, Spider, Filipino, Black and White Ringtails, Cinnamon, Owl Face Monkeys and South American Ringtails were some of the monkey types who were calling Coxville their home.

Junior seemed to be the public's favorite, and it was easy to tell that they wanted to reward Junior by giving him some treats. I really didn't have anything appropriate for customers to feed Junior, so I decided to get some peanuts. I bought 100 pounds of unroasted peanuts in the shell. My next purchase was for a popcorn machine so I could keep the peanuts hot and also sell popcorn.

Once, the routine of letting Junior mingle with visitors backfired on me. It started out like most December days in Texas when temperatures are often mild. I had Junior out frolicking around in the area he loved best, where he could do some rock climbing. He was harnessed and visiting with the public. Then I got involved with a customer and turned my back on him. It had been less than ten minutes when I went back to visit with him, but much to my surprise, he was missing......harness and all! Junior was kidnapped on December 23, 1946. It looked like our Christmas was not going to be all that jolly after all.

We ran the following article in the LOST AND FOUND column along with Junior's picture in the Austin newspaper:

LOST AND FOUND

PLEASE HELP find Junior, 4 lb. monkey, $50 for his return. Stolen by a soldier hitchhiking north from Austin, December 23. Last seen in Round Rock, supposed to be going to Chicago. Soldier has been bitten on hand by monkey. Phone 8-993 or write Coxville, Austin, Texas.

Customers asked about him and felt the loss just about as much as our family did. Somehow, we made it through the Christmas holidays without the little fellow. Little did we know then that the New Year was going to be an especially good one for us. Junior returned home after spending ten days in the Army on the base at Fort Hood, Texas.

After life was back to normal again with Junior home, I got to thinking one day that Junior ought to have a wife. It was time to spread the word to my customers, friends and vendors that I was looking for another monkey.

A food snack salesman that called on me remarked one day that he found a monkey up in Georgetown and that the owner was anxious to get rid of it. I said "Gosh, how much is it?" He said he thought $15.00. I tried to give him $15.00 and he said "No, if I get the monkey, I'll bring it to you and then you can pay me."

Sure enough, late one afternoon, he came driving in. He said: "Come and get this monkey out of the back of my truck". I followed him out and looking inside the truck I saw bags and bags of potato chips scattered all around. I offered to pay for the damaged goods but he said, "Never mind, these are the stale chips I just picked up".

So now we had two monkeys and it just so happened that the newly purchased monkey was a Rhesus monkey and that the first one I had was a Capuchin monkey, but both of them were males.

These two particular monkeys were really gentle and were allowed a lot of freedom out of their cages with Coxville visitors who could pet and photograph them. They made everyone laugh and forget their personal problems. They were truly great entertainers.

Soon the Coxville family welcomed another Rhesus monkey that had quite a history. His previous owner had a motorcycle and the monkey got to ride along with him. After we adopted him at the zoo, he slipped out while I was cleaning his cage. He got on top of the monkey house that had been built especially for him. Knowing that Rhesus monkeys could be very temperamental and hard to handle, I began to plot and plan the best method to lure him back to his cage. At that time, I had an old 1935 model Chevrolet with a bad muffler. Remembering how much the monkey had enjoyed riding on a motorcycle with his previous owner, I started racing the motor to make a lot of noise. Then I began to call the monkey to come to me while I was sitting in the Chevy with the window rolled down.

Believe it or not, it worked! The monkey jumped right into the car and then I quickly rolled up the windows. After going for a little joy ride together, the monkey allowed me to return him to his cage.

Josie

Another Rhesus monkey with an unbelievable personality was Josie. She enjoyed looking at herself in the mirror provided to her. She would make faces at herself, grin, and try to keep her teeth clean by rubbing them with a paper towel or anything else she could find in her cage that might aid her in maintaining her beautiful smile.

Linus

Then we acquired Linus, a white-faced monkey, who spent most of his days, enjoying himself as he wandered around on a leash attached to a pole. Linus got his name because he loved his blanket. Whenever an airplane would fly nearby, he would get his blanket and immediately cover-up his head. If we tried to separate him from his "blankie", he would throw a temper tantrum.

Linus, like all animals, had his own unique personality. Some of the memories that I fondly remember of him were that he loved to drink cold drinks from a bottle.

Linus had a favorite playmate which was a terrier dog. Linus was a smart little guy and enjoyed providing for his friend's needs. He would reach for the water faucet to turn it on and off whenever he wanted to refill the dog's water bowl. Linus also liked to wear a sweater during the cool days of autumn and winter.

"Twelve monkeys in the bathroom one cold winter when my electric heaters went out almost made my wife desert me. Just one of the problems that was common to the operation of the privately owned zoo."

Photo by William E. Lummus

*And now as author, this story continues to unfold
from what my Dad and Mother
shared with me over the years ...*

The hobby grew by leaps and bounds and by 1948, the animal collection had grown to 500 birds and animals. Nearly all animals that most public zoos had were now at Coxville. Exceptions would be large jungle animals such as elephants, rhinos, giraffes, hippos, etc. Nearly all the animals that were adopted had names, most often the name of the donor. There were sixteen monkeys keeping tourists entertained for free with their antics behind bars. All of the monkeys had names and if the former owner's had named them, those names were kept for these new pets.

But....there was going to be even more excitement in the Cox family in 1948 because that's when I enter their lives...

A Very Special Birthday in 1948

My mother and dad, Alvin and Doris had decided it was time to add a large bedroom, a larger living area, and hall to the house as they had planned to add another member to the family. This time, however, it would not be a furry monkey, but instead a baby sister for Darlene. It would be ME!

Alvin's special day, his birthday was July 10th. But in 1948, on a Saturday, that day became even more special. At 1:24 p.m., Doris presented Alvin with a very special birthday present, another baby girl, named Denise. Alvin immediately presented Doris with pink carnations. Dad and I shared a special bond throughout our lives and made a great effort to celebrate most every birthday together.

Apparently, when I was 18 months old, I went with my Dad to help feed the horses. Mom's last words as we walked out the door that day were "Alvin, just be careful and make sure you watch her!" At that time, they had two quarter horse mares, Jet and Flash, one with a filly. Lots of things can happen in a split second and as Dad began feeding, I walked too close to the mare that had the colt.

The mare kicked me, but I just rolled and rolled. Dad told me later that when he asked me if I was hurt, I said "No, but I'm dirty!" I was covered with burrs. It just so happened that I was so close to the mares' back legs that my body didn't realize the full impact of the kick and that's all that could have saved me from being seriously injured. Needless to say, Dad was too nervous to take me along again for some time. As an adult, I still don't like to get dirty!

As children we enjoyed the experience of nursing baby fawns. Mom and Dad showed us how to fill a Coca-Cola bottle with milk and attached a black nipple when we were just barely three years old. We were all fascinated with watching the "spots" disappear as they little fawns matured.

The Cox daughters developed a love
for animals at a very early age.

Alvin said that in 1952, the family needed a rest and change of pace so they rented out the station for two years. It was a happy two years and Alvin now had two young daughters and a wife to enjoy. It was decided that Alvin would enlarge the small house that his parents previously lived in. Manford and Bertha Cox, his parents, would move to the small, but adequate living quarters in the rear of the service station building. His parents were raising Pekinese and Chihuahua dogs and had as many as fifty at one time before they began selling them. They sold them about as quickly as they could get them registered and ready for their new owners.

During these two years, a major expansion took place of the zoo as more pens and cages for the animals were built as they continued to care for them each day. Doris went to the library and brought home lots of reference books and referred to the "World Book" encyclopedias often so that she and Alvin could learn about all the different types of monkeys and chimpanzees too. Even though they didn't have a chimpanzee yet, they were already making plans to get one.

The fifty-six acres now consisted of seven efficiency cabins and were rented on a monthly basis to University students who had meager incomes, often with the wife working and the husband going to school. Housing close in was too costly and not too much was available since Austin was still not growing very fast. Several couples stayed there for four years and the Cox family became very interested and involved in their schooling. The Cox's kept in touch with several of them for years to come. The Coxes rented one place to a semi-retired couple and another to their son and young bride. These families stayed on Coxville property until children came along and they needed more living space.

Business was growing, so another baby was planned, hoping they might have a son. However, they lost this baby at four months and the doctor advised Doris to wait one year before trying to have another since she was then 36 years of age.

Deedra Jean Cox (nicknamed D.D.) was born on August 12, 1958, almost two years later, when Doris was 38. Ten years between daughters proved to be both challenging and rewarding. When Deedra was four months old, they lifted their belongings over the fence and moved into a new, larger brick home with three bedrooms and two baths. Times had really changed.

Coxville had lots of animals including lots of monkeys in 1958, but Alvin had always wanted a chimpanzee. After Deedra was born, they decided it was time to locate one.

Patsy

Patsy was a chimpanzee that liked to dress up. Alvin had an old hat that she found one day and even though she was quite ladylike, she enjoyed wearing his hat. She would wear clothes and parade around on a leash when visitors came.

Patsy, Bertha, Deedra, and Manford Cox

If Patsy escaped from Alvin's arms, she would head for our home and Doris would open the door. She learned quickly the benefits of jumping into Doris' arms and receiving a special treat and some tender loving conversation. If she went to the house and none of the family happened to be home then she would climb up the old oak tree out front and wait until Alvin came after her. If she wasn't quite ready to come down, he would have to get the water hose to sprinkle her with a shower until she got thoroughly drenched. She would then descend from the tree and she'd jump into his arms. The next step would be to put dry clothes on her.

Patsy with best friend and playmate "D.D".

When Alvin took her out of the cage in the morning, he would give her a paper towel and say "Patsy, clean up now for your breakfast." She would clean her hands, wipe the cage and then hold out her hand. He'd give her some warm coffee with sugar. Anyone observing could quickly tell by the look on her face that she thoroughly enjoyed her coffee! When the coffee cup was about empty, she would take her fingers and get the rest of the sugar out from the bottom of the cup. After she finished her morning cup, Alvin would hand her another clean-up towel and she would clean her sticky fingers. When people would buy cold drinks, she would hold out a cup hoping they'd share and sometimes she would be lucky enough to receive a refill. She also enjoyed looking at herself in a mirror.

After the monkeys, along came more animals and Alvin soon learned that he needed to build a lot more cages to house them in. The monkeys at Coxville were to become one of the star attractions with young and old visitors for years to come at the zoo.

It was a challenge for Alvin to find the best living arrangements for each specific animal. Some needed to be in an environment filled with trees to climb, acorns and leaves to munch on and/or shade to lounge beneath. Many animals in the zoo (bears, raccoons, javelins, and deer) enjoyed the acorns from the abundance of oak trees on the Coxville property. A lot of the new residents were going to require much greater security.

Alvin hired a man to help him build cages and he said, "You can build cages if you learn how to weld", so he was kind enough to teach Alvin this trade. Alvin used some concrete blocks, water troughs, feed bowls and built dens so when the Mama Lion had babies she would have a private den where she could take care of her young cubs. When he boarded some animals for the winter months, he now had round concrete, heavy wire cages with individual runs for monkeys. Coxville had heaters for the cold months and an inside area where the caretaker could go to clean and feed from the back of each cage.

Alvin's reputation in the Austin area was that he would take just about any animal in and give it a home. Every animal in the zoo became special and acquired a personal name. At mealtime, one of our family discussions often revolved about what we should name a new member of the Coxville family.

The zookeeper enjoyed interacting with his customers of all ages. He was never "at a loss for words" and enjoyed talking about his animals like most parents talk about their children. It seemed he never met a stranger. If Alvin Cox had a spare moment, he would offer to wrap a snake around your neck and let you have that rare experience to remember for years to come. The zoo offered pony and pony cart rides for the children and peanuts to feed the monkeys.

At one time, there was even a service station and garage for repairs located on these fifty-six acres of property. Children as well as the "young at heart" enjoyed the entertainment that the animals in the Coxville Zoo provided for the quarter entrance fee.   There were animals to make your laugh and forget your troubles.

This little fawn gets a second chance at life with a new mother after it was left motherless when his real mom was shot accidentally by a hunter.

Sometimes visitors would get to experience holding a baby lion cub; pet Tabu the tiger who could be seen at times intermingling with the public; or give a baby fawn some bottled milk.

More often than not, when someone brought Alvin an animal it was because its mother had disappeared leaving the babies to fend for themselves.

Soldiers, sailors, and Marines that were stationed on various islands during the war would many times return with a pet, but often their wife or mother did not take too kindly to having a monkey to care for, so Coxville acquired quite a few "would-be home-breakers" and gave them a residence.

St. Louis Zoo advertised they had some lion cubs for sale so Coxville ordered a pair, but soon discovered that we had two females.   When contacted again to order a male, they stated that they did not have any at that time.   The Coxes called Buckhorn Drive-In Theatre as neighbors heard that they had animals available for sale.   A trucker friend furnished Coxville his truck, and Alvin filled it with gas and drove to Mission, Texas.   Alvin came home with one male and one female grown lion, a Coati Mundi, red fox, raccoons and several other small animals.

Coxville had red and gray foxes. They were nocturnal residents of the zoo who had a keen sense of sight, hearing and smell. They were shy, but curious and very playful animals.

Later, a friend found a mama fox and gave her and five babies to the zoo. They were placed in a pen that night, and we soon found out just how intelligent she was because the next morning, we found out she had dug out of the pen deserting her babies (pups).

Doris with Mama Fox

We now had an immediate need to learn how to care for these youngsters. We already had a pen that was vacant, so we placed a hollow stump in it so they could make themselves at home. We fed these particular animals a diet of mice, chicken necks, fruit and corn. There was an oak tree that shaded the pen, and we soon learned how much they enjoyed the acorns that fell into their cage.

Photo by William E. Lummus

The raccoon, a nocturnal resident, has acute senses and their eyes are well adapted to the dark. Their front paws are not webbed and they use them with great dexterity when they handle food or open garbage cans looking for food. Raccoons are omnivores and they love sweet corn, potatoes, peas and most other vegetables and fruits such as peaches, plums or berries.

There were pet raccoons at Coxville as well as the many wild raccoons that naturally inhabited the area along with the snakes, porcupines, coyotes, opossums, armadillos, and porcupines in this central Texas area.   It was important to provide a home for each of these natural habitants at Coxville because lots of visitors came during Christmas or summer breaks to see animals that they did not commonly see in their own states and were always interested in knowing more about these critters.

Another fascinating resident native to this Texas area is the porcupine. It has a round body, short legs, small ears and relatively small head that are covered with black to brownish-yellow fur. It is part of the rodent family and is an herbivore because it eats leaves, twigs and green plants.   It likes to climb trees and is mostly nocturnal. Porcupines enjoy eating many kinds of trees and woody shrubs. They like to gnaw on wood objects and are attracted by salt. In fact, they are responsible for chewing on tool handles found in many barns and sheds. These particular handles attract them because they have salt deposits left on them from human sweat.

The porcupine is an excellent swimmer because its hollow quills help keep it afloat. It is a very vocal animal that makes moaning, grunting, whining, shrieking and tooth clicking sounds.

The porcupine is most known because it may have as many as 30,000 quills.   The quills cover all of its body except for the stomach and the longest quills are on its rump while the shortest are on its cheeks. Baby porcupines are called "porcupettes" and are born with soft quills that harden about an hour after birth.

Contrary to what a lot of people believe, the porcupine cannot shoot its quills at a predator while trying to defend himself.

The porcupine uses its quills to defend itself from predators such as coyotes, owls, bobcats, mountain lions and wolves. The quills come out of the porcupine's skin easily and become embedded deeper and deeper in the predator's skin which is very painful and can even be fatal.

Believe it or not, a very common critter in Texas that is often spotted in the wild became a favorite at the zoo. The opossum captivated many visitors because the female has an external fur-lined abdominal pouch for carrying her young. The premature embryos leave the womb and crawl to the pouch. The young are extremely tiny, blind, and incomplete in development. In fact, it takes 22-24 newborns to equal the weight of a penny. They are weaned in 75-80 days. As they grow up, they cling to their mother's fur and ride on her back just like you see in the photo on the next page.

The opossum is the size of a domestic house cat but has shorter legs and a heavier body. It eats just about anything including fruits, berries, small mammals, birds, eggs and insects.

It is known to "feign death" (playing possum) which is induced by fear and stress. In this state, it appears unconscious, the mouth opens slightly, and the entire body becomes limp.

Once when I was about 6 years old, I was visiting my grandparents, Wade and Myrtle Hunsucker in Staples, Texas. Pa-Paw took me out in the cotton field on a typical summer day with temperatures well into the upper 90's. I remember he always wore his straw hat and long sleeved shirt and Ma-Maw wore her homemade bonnet and long dress made out of flour sack material to shield the sun's rays. My grandfather came across an opossum as we were all walking up and down the rows. He wanted to chase the varmint away so it wouldn't mess with his crop, so he hit it on the head with a shovel. I always loved animals and immediately gave "Pa-Paw" a bad time for hitting the animal. He laughed and said "You can't really kill them." He wanted to show the theory of "playing possum" with this pest so he took some dried stalks from his cotton field and proceeded to cover the little rascal. I was extremely curious about what he was going to do next. I observed him removing his cigarette lighter from his shirt pocket. Then he lit a small fire on top of the stalks. Immediately the opossum took off "lickety-split" across the field. When I was satisfied that the newly found critter was indeed all right, we returned to the front screened porch of their house for sweetened iced tea, cookies and a game of dominos.

This shows a mother opossum who, at one time, was a tenant at the beloved Coxville Zoo. The opossum is not a very lovely animal, but she was a good mother to her little one. I found as a photographer, that she was one of the best!

Photo and comment by William E. Lummus

Two common animals had an unusual occurrence at Coxville as there was a mother cat that adopted skunk babies and fed them until they could eat on their own. Our family got to keep one baby skunk for a pet and she was as gentle as the mother cat. She slept in a little bathtub and romped and played with us.

Cats make amazing mothers, and one particular black cat we had nursed baby skunks just like they were her own kittens.

Photo by William E. Lummus

Native Americans gave this strange animal the Abenaki (Algonquian) Indian name "seganku" which meals "one who squirts". They spray or "squirt" as part of the self-defense since they may only weigh six to fourteen pounds.

They have two scent glands near the base of their tails and each one is surrounded by muscle tissue that can contract to spray fine yellow droplets fifteen feet or more. Besides the penetrating odor, it can cause temporary blindness or nausea to anyone that is in the path of the spray. Most people use tomato juice to mask the odor, but we heard that the best way to remove the odor was to mix a solution of hydrogen peroxide with a quarter cup of baking soda and a teaspoon of liquid dishwashing soap.

Skunks are most active in late evening and early hours of the night but do move about during the day. They prefer meat but will eat plants and vegetation. If they could pick their favorite smorgasbord, it would consist primarily of insects, grasshoppers, birds, worms, eggs, berries and grubs, but love honey, molasses, and peanut butter on bread. Skunks are a member of the weasel family which includes minks, fishers, and otters.

The baby skunk shown above was found in the woods near Austin, Texas, not far from its dead mother. It was brought into camp by some hunters and introduced to the mother cat shown with it. The cat immediately adopted the baby skunk and seemed just as proud of it as if it were her own baby. This is one of my favorite photos.

Comment and Photo by William E. Lummus

Next, Coxville got a hyena. This was an unusual animal for our area and many people had never seen one. Since little was known about them by our family, we had to research information to learn how to feed and house it.

The hyena looks like a rather large dog and their front legs are actually longer than their back legs that allow them to stalk and chase their prey for miles and miles at about 6 mph until their victims become exhausted from being chased. They have a heart that is twice the size of an adult lion which makes them very strong and able to actually move at speeds of up to 30 mph.

It didn't take us long to understand why they were often referred to as the "laughing" hyena as they made a very loud giggling sound when they got excited. We could hear them all the way from our home even though the hyena was at the far end of the zoo by the entrance. Our family knew firsthand that any kind of vehicle with a siren going down North Lamar Boulevard in front of Coxville would cause the hyenas to "laugh" very loudly!

Hyenas are very intelligent, and some scientists claim that their intelligence is equal to certain apes. This is another reason why they are such calculated hunters.

Hyenas are mainly nocturnal, and for the most part, the females dominated the males. Communication was very important to them and they made vocal sounds in addition to the "laughing" sounds that sounded like squeals, whines, growls, grunts and roars. They are scavengers and hunt for their own food in their natural environment; eating the leftovers of other animals.

We were amazed to know that the hyena's bite pressure could reach 800 lbs. per inch which could certainly crush a bone. This explained why there was no "clean-up" necessary for me to do after the hyena's meals; they ate everything including the bones!

Next, our family heard there was a bear in Amarillo that would be killed if they could not find a home for him. So Alvin went to pick him up in White Deer, Texas (near Amarillo). After several hours of coaxing that "rascal", the bear was loaded in a cage in the back of Coxville's pickup truck.

After that we added black swans, white swans, geese, and Chinese Sulkies (native oriental chickens with hair instead of feathers. We used these birds to hatch gold and silver pheasant eggs at Coxville. Peacocks and pigeons added to our collection. The male peacocks strutted about and would bring sighs from the visitors when they spread their colorful tail feathers. Red, white and blue pigeons added a patriotic color scheme.

Other animals residing in the Coxville Zoo were: Shetland ponies, horses, cows, peacocks, white herons, pelicans, a Mexican lion, wolves, monkeys, red and yellow parrots, ducks, ringtail cats, squirrels, lynx cats, bobcats, parakeets, deer, pigeons, Snookum bear (Coati), white rats, guinea pigs, Persian and Siamese cats, lions, coyotes, goats, fish, turtles, terrapins, macaws, myna birds, ringtail doves, speckled civet cat, striped pole cat, javelins or wild hogs, many kinds of snakes including albino rattlesnakes, baboons, bears, opossums, rabbits, armadillos, and (55 Pekingese and Chihuahua dogs in 1948). Many animals came from Snake King in Brownsville.

The public was free to feed the animals as all the expenses involved to feed and maintain the zoo animals had to come from the Coxes. Alvin Cox loved his business and hobby but it was definitely a costly venture.

Since the City of Austin did not have a zoo, many people visited Coxville because they were not able to take trips to San Antonio, Dallas, Houston, or elsewhere to see animals.

For many years the zoo was free to the public and then later donation cans were placed at the entrance to the zoo. An average collection would consist of about twelve to thirty dollars a week.

When Interstate Highway 35 was built, business took a nosedive. A pay gate was installed and a quarter was set as an entrance fee. But Alvin was soft hearted and could never keep from unlocking the gate to allow anyone who could not afford the fee to see the animals and enjoy his hobby. The turn style gate itself was quite an endeavor to build and Alvin bought the materials, designed it and constructed it in his spare time.

Cecil

The next acquisition at Coxville was an eighteen-inch long alligator from a serviceman that had been on maneuvers in Louisiana. When he returned home with this alligator for a pet, his wife didn't take kindly to the idea and he couldn't keep it. He was named "Cecil" after the serviceman that gave it to the zoo.

The photograph of "Old Lockjaw" shows a baby alligator hitching a ride on "Old Lockjaw's" back. They were great friends at the Coxville Zoo. This is just one more proof of the most unusual friendships that lived and flourished at Austin's beloved Coxville Zoo!

Photo and comment by William E. Lummus

About thirty years later, the alligator was over six feet long. It had spent many years savoring the flavors of fish and fresh chicken necks. The chicken necks were purchased for a quarter in two-gallon buckets from a famous chicken restaurant on North Lamar called the Chicken Shack.

One beautiful afternoon, Dad set me up with a cane pole and I took off fishing in our lake with one of my girlfriends. When the catch was brought home to cook, Mother decided that the fish was just too little to cook and would be better fed to the alligators for a snack. I wanted to feed them to docile-looking Cecil who almost always seemed lazy and barely moved about from the water to his landing where he enjoyed his daily sunbaths. To protect the zoo visitors and the alligators, Dad designed and built a chain-linked fence to surround the alligator pond and sundeck. Somehow Cecil caught a whiff of the fishy smell, and as I stuck the fish through the fence to drop it down into the water, he leaped out of the water and over to the fence and promptly removed the fish completely out of my fingers' grasp. Boy was I ever surprised! I had never seen an alligator move so rapidly and thought he was going to swallow my fingers along with the fish. Another memory I'll always have with me!

Alligators have broad, flat, and rounded snouts, as opposed to the longer, sharper snouts of other crocodilians. Unlike crocodilians, their lower teeth cannot be seen when their mouths are closed. Alligators have a third (transparent) eyelid that gives them underwater protection.

As an adult, now living in West Palm Beach, Florida, my younger sister, Deedra says that one of the things she enjoyed as a daughter of a zookeeper was watching Dad interact with the alligators. She recalls him feeding them lots of chicken necks and fresh fish. As daughters, we enjoyed a small "plastic" swimming pool in our yard, but the alligators had a much larger cement pool where they could spend their time laying around lazily either on the sundeck area or in the cool waters. Deedra remembers that many zoo visitors did not realize that the alligators were in fact alive. When anyone tossed fresh fish over the fence, the gators would leap out of the water and catch them in their big jaws, splash back down in the water, and soak all of the visitors nearby with a bath.

Visitors were amazed that our dad went in the pen to clean out their pool, only carrying a water hose, bleach, and a broom. Though he had a healthy respect for the animals, he never seemed afraid of any of them. If the alligators started to slide down into the pool while he was standing in it to clean it, he would simply remind them with a touch from the broom to their snout and "sweet talk" them back up on the deck.

He had to drain their pool to let out the old water before filling it with fresh and when he did so, special treasures of alligator teeth could be found on the ground below. Visitors and each of the daughters would collect the teeth. All three Cox daughters enjoyed taking them to school for "Show and Tell" for their classmates. Alligators have eighty teeth, forty on the top and forty on the bottom; their teeth are conical and used for grabbing and holding, not for cutting. Young alligators can replace teeth every year or so.

Alligators build brushy round dome shaped nests out of existing material. Digging a hole into the center of the dome, she lays her eggs, covers them with leaves and brush, and allows the natural heat to aid in the incubation of the eggs. She stands guard over the nest to protect the eggs from predators so that they will not dig them up and eat them.

When the eggs are ready to hatch, in about 60 days, the young begin to croak softly within the egg. Baby alligators are equipped with an egg tooth (a toughened bit of epidermis on the tip of the hatchling's nose which allows them to break out of their egg).

The Creeps

One of the most intriguing and unique acquisitions was an Iguana who quickly made himself comfortable in his new zoo surroundings. Shortly after, another type of lizard, the Gila (heel-uh) Monster related to an Iguana, joined the zoo family.

Doris enjoyed the majority of the zoo family, but the Gila Monster "gave her the creeps". This is a large lizard (oviparous – meaning they lay eggs) that is poisonous with a purple forked tongue. It is covered with knobby scales called tubercles. Lizards are cold blooded and must control their body temperature by seeking sun or shade. They like to eat eggs of snakes and birds. They also like to eat small ground squirrels, rabbits and birds.

Alvin put the Gila Monster in a giant aquarium and added rocks, plants and sand (where they could dig holes to lay their eggs). It was equally important to have a large container of water because they often liked to just lie in it.

The Gila Monster was most active in April and May and then would rest in the hot summer (called aestivation). And then when the fall months approached, it would become active again until the winter hibernation.

Interestingly, their tail is a food storage bin which allows their hibernation in the winter because they have stored fat in their tail during the times they are actively eating.

Coxville also had an Iguana Lizard from South America. It was pretty vicious looking and had to be kept really warm in the winter. He was put in a big box with a screen cover and brought into the warm garage to winter.

The success of my father's collecting soon grew into the favorite destination for local Austin field trips, family outings and neighborhood children. The various animals captured the attention of young and old who visited to amuse themselves by observing and interacting with the animals at Coxville.

WHY Coxville?

It's all about the...

KIDS and the CRITTERS

Neighbor/Cowboy Chan Snyder

Denise, Half-Pint, Alvin and a lion cub

Alvin with a gentle Shetland and a zoo visitor

Jimmy's drawing of the "monkey house".

Fun at the ZOO!

"Animals will bite "written underneath
Walter's drawing of a "LOIN".

A baby raccoon.

ROOM 107

On May 24, 1965 Walnut Creek School in Austin Texas wrote:

"Thank-you for letting us go to Coxville. It was very nice of you. Thank-you for the candy and balloons."

A ninth grade student named Jeanie Beal wrote the following essay in Mrs. Johnson's English class in 1952 and sent it to Alvin and M. J. Cox:

"Coxville Zoo, so-called because Mr. Al Cox and his son own it, is situated among a huge clump of trees on the Dallas Highway. To get there from Congress Avenue and Eleventh Street, you turn left and go on up to Guadalupe Street, where you turn right. Continue on Guadalupe the rest of the way out there. The name of Guadalupe changes to North Highway, or Dallas Highway. After reaching the city limits, go four miles further, and look for Coxville Zoo on the left side of the highway. The charge for entering is twenty-five cents for an adult and ten cents for children. If you are unable to pay, you may visit free of charge.

As you enter, you will probably hear nearly every kind of noise imaginable that an animal can make, because there are over five hundred different kinds of birds and animals, ranging from monkeys, bears, and alligators, to lovebirds, birds of paradise, and hens from Africa. Some of these birds, such as the one of paradise and the peacock, are so beautiful that a few Indians come to the zoo every year, at opening of spring, and gather up their shed feathers which they highly prize and adore.

The unique zoo was started as a hobby in 1939, and the first animal was a monkey. The monkey started out as a household pet of the Coxes, and became one of the much-stared-at animals in the zoo.

Beside the zoo, there is a beautiful rock garden, built as a hobby by Mr. and Mrs. M. J. Cox. Mrs. Cox was interested in building small size houses, and modeling things out of clay. As a result, she has built a "little city" surrounding a fish pond. Mr. Cox helped her build the school house, with a teacher and children all around it, a railroad station with toy tracks and train, a house with a manger scene, a home, and people everywhere. In the back of the little city are the natural rock formations. These rocks have been found all over the United States and brought back to Coxville. You have to use your imagination a bit, but you can find bears, mermaids, squirrels, dogs, rats, and anything else you would like to imagine in the Rock Garden.

There have been quite a few generous people who have given animals to the zoo. An oil man once gave a mountain lion, and a man with at traveling show gave a baboon. There is one little boy in Austin who boards his monkey out there during the winter, and takes him back home during the summer, when the monkey can stay outside, because his mother doesn't like to have it in the house. People who have found large turtles have often given them to the zoo, also.

Many improvements have been added since the zoo began its life thirteen years ago. Cages for the wild monkeys and baboons were built about three years ago. Huge cages for the lions and a large pool for the alligators were added six months ago.

Jeanie's essay continued to point out the sign that was posted at the zoo's entrance which read:

STOP AND THINK!

The nickel and dime that you drop in for donation can buy food for these animals. These animals eat in one week; 374 pounds of meat, two barrels of bread, 100 pounds horse meat, and mule feed, 224 bananas, 100 pounds of chicken scratch, grapes, peanuts, honey, cakes, cookies, and many other things. This private zoo was started as a hobby in 1939. I have bought most of these animals, and built cages for them. I give most of my time caring for them. So don't forget the donation cans on each side of the gate.

Thank you,

A. W. and M. J. COX"

(Even though Dad relished having visitors, he realized the rising costs and appealed to them for a little contribution.)

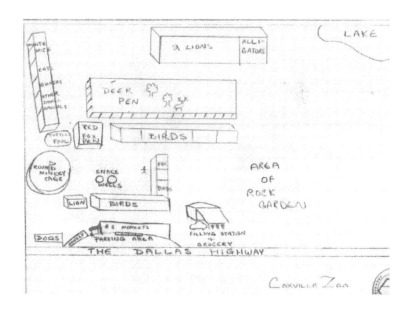

A student's map of Coxville

During the 1940's, 1950's and early 1960's, there weren't computers, water slides, or theme parks, so the number of things that the whole family could enjoy as an outing for free was limited.

Coxville Gardens was worth a trip to see but there were also other attractions there. Coxville had cabins, a tourist court, and a lake house for rent and there was another one of my favorite places to go which was...

COXVILLE LAKE

There was a small spring-fed creek running through the back of our business. The Coxes built a large dam and it was 16 feet deep in some places. Thus, Coxville Lake was created. It was stocked with catfish, bream, bass and other fish. There was a charge of half a dollar to fish for half a day and a one-dollar would get you a whole day of fishing. Small canoes were allowed in the Coxville Lake.

*Alvin caught dinner for the family
and some of the zoo animals too!*

If you were one of the early birds to arrive at Coxville Lake, you might even luck out and get to use the boat.

Curley Clark shows off his catch of the day

One of the most fortunate occurrences for the zoo came with the opportunity for appearances on The "Uncle Jay Show"

The Uncle Jay Show was a local television show that aired in Austin on KTBC's channel 7 about 4:00 p.m. on weekdays. Austin children were told they could bring pets or other items for the "show and tell" segment of the program. Darlene and Denise had baby lion cubs for pets and took them on one show and made quite a hit.

Darlene, Denise and Lion Cubs

"Jay" asked the girls where they got the little cubs and they told him that their Daddy had a zoo at Coxville. They were asked if their Dad could bring some other animals for the viewers to see.

On April 13, 1956, the Cox family received one of their favorite letters from Mrs. Albert O' Daniel of Austin, Texas. Excerpts from her letter were:

"I just this minute got through watching you and your darling daughters on Uncle Jay's program. I always watch the program on Wednesday afternoons and if I do happen to miss it, I wonder what you had on it. I believe today topped them all though with the assortment of baby animals, chickens, and etc."

       She went on to write, "When I see the little lion cubs, my hands just tingle to cuddle them. They are so cute. All in all your appearance with the little animals just adds a touch of that something special to our local TV. I was brought up on a farm and wanted you to know that others like me knew what a big chore it was to care for those animals. I just want you to know that my family and myself (my son is 22), all love and enjoy the efforts you put forth to bring such a fine program to the little children as well as we adults."

       Her P.S. was: "This is the first fan letter I ever wrote."

So for several years, once a week, Dad took animals for children to enjoy as they watched this television show.

Allowing his sense of humor to surface, Alvin once came up with a crazy idea to put a goose in a Sinclair plastic "blow-up" toy that was supposed to be a dinosaur. Deedra was about three years old at the time and really got a kick out of it, so Alvin took the idea to the Uncle Jay Show to show the other youngsters in the viewing area. It was amazing how many people called or came out to Coxville, believing that there really was a baby dinosaur living there!

Alvin took a fawn, a fox, different kinds of snakes, raccoons, albino skunks, parrots, a coati mundi, an iguana, turtles, a baby alligator and of course, Black Cherry, his smallest Shetland pony to the show for the Austin children to see.

Llama Lisa Loved Llama Louie

Llamas are members of the camel family and among the world's oldest domestic animals. A mature llama makes a great pack animal and can carry from 70 – 100 pounds for long distances. Because llamas are very sociable herd animals, Alvin knew that he had to get his first llama a companion as soon as he could locate one. It didn't take long for Llama Louie and Llama Lisa to become "soul mates".

Llamas are gentle and have a calm nature. They have a three-compartment stomach like cattle and sheep and chew their cud. They generally live from fifteen to twenty-nine years and weigh anywhere from 200 to 450 pounds each.

Llamas will spit at other llamas in order to establish the pecking order of the group. It is easy to tell when they are getting ready to spit as they will usually tilt their heads back, point their nose up in the air, and pull their ears back. It is their way of saying "knock it off"! The picture below features Alvin Cox with Llama Lisa in 1967.

I will return this narration back now to Dad as he continues telling you how his passion continues and how his vision widens for his beloved animals...

Alvin loved to tell how he acquired 101 Shetland Ponies!

The first Shetland pony I bought was in 1950. My dad, Manford Cox had visited a place near Denton and had seen a pony that he wanted shipped to his granddaughters. It was very cold that December and the pony was exposed to extreme temperatures during shipment. Unfortunately, he took pneumonia and was not able to recover from this illness. Still wanting a pony for our daughters and for the zoo, we located two mares which were from thirty-two to thirty-four inches tall, and a stallion from another source. So we began raising Shetlands by breeding the brown mare, Bunny and the red and white paint, Cleo to Timmy. Timmy was a frisky dapple gray stud with a white mane and tail. As a result, the first colts born to Coxville were named Trixie and Danny.

Our pony herd grew quickly as I acquired stock from as far away as Tennessee and Texas cities of Temple, Killeen and Denton. In addition, we had six to eight new colts born every year. I sold some over the years, but had a hard time letting any of them "leave home". When I decided to get out of the pony business in 1970, I had 101 ponies and each and every one had been given a special name by someone in our family. The girls enjoying helping us come up with the new names such as: Gumdrop, Silver, Chestnut, Raven, Marvel, Slow Poke, Princess, Pet, Rocky, Trigger, Dottie, Cyclone, Dixie, Gypsy, May Day, and Black Cherry.

Timmy, our thirty-four inch virile stud Shetland thought that all the mares in the herd belonged in his harem. For awhile things were going his way, but as usual all good things must come to an end and along came Half-Pint, a twenty-nine inch stud that joined the herd. He too thought that he was at least ten feet tall and decided that he should now be the "king" of the herd. We always had to keep the two in different stalls or fields so that they would not fight. Occasionally they would get through a fence and have a battle. I believe that if I had not been able to separate them, one of them would have killed the other for breeding rights. Half-Pint had a broad back and was very strong, but ever so gentle with the children.

One day in August, the Texas temperatures warmed up well over 100 degrees and Denise went down to the barn to help feed the ponies. Denise got into a position where she backed up too close to the gate of the stall where Timmy was housed. Timmy and Half-Pint were pretty excited about a new mare we had added. Timmy was blind but that never kept him from chasing or competing with Half-Pint for the mares. He picked up Half-Pint's scent on Denise and took a rather large bite out of her middle back. When Timmy bit and released Denise, the impact knocked her into a mound of horse manure. She cried but I don't think it was all pain that she was suffering. She was pretty humiliated that she had been thrown into a pile of manure and thought she had been ruined for life. She had only a little sun suit on at the time, so the tooth marks remained a long time reminding her of this incident.

I had two quarter horse mares, Flash and Jet, sired at King's Ranch. We bred them to the Shetland studs by artificial insemination. When grown, these were forty-two inch ponies. These colts were able to accommodate the larger children who wanted to ride them for a longer time. Some of the colts they had were named Dusty, Red Sands, Comet, Rocket, Venus, Firecracker, Lightning, Red Pepper, and Thunder and Plain Jane.

Not long after, a man from Oklahoma brought me another pony. This was one of the smallest stallions I had ever seen. It was black, good-natured, and very gentle. He was named "Half-Pint". The mares and the little colts were about the size of a large dog weighing about 40 pounds. Black Cherry had a beautiful white star and was to be the smallest pony ever born at Coxville. Black Cherry's parents were Half-Pint and Raven.

I used him to breed my mares and had a number of really small ponies about 29 inches tall. No matter how many new ponies were born or acquired over the years, Half-Pint quickly worked his way into my heart and would always be my favorite Shetland pony.

Alvin and Half-Pint with visitors

I built a "pony cart" and he ever so proudly pulled the children around the walkways, trotting along. He lived to be an old, old pony as so many of my animals did due to the tender, loving care that I and my family provided.

Most Sundays, our family enjoyed lunch usually complete with homemade lemon or butterscotch pies after the girls attended Sunday school at the First Methodist Church. Then the afternoons were primarily dedicated to running the "pony ride". We charged each rider a quarter. My daughters got to keep all the quarters as allowance for working the rides and doing the chores involved. The quarter price was fixed for over ten years while the pony rides ran for the children at the zoo.

I built a pony ride for six riders. One of the young boys that I had employed to help at Coxville would help my daughters' saddle up the ponies and get them ready for the riders. The pony ride helped train the ponies and taught them to lead and follow, stop on command, and get used to children. Later I increased the rides to a dozen. I bought my saddles from Mexico and always got a few extras so I would have one to sell whenever I sold one as a pet to a family. I put a breast harness on the stud, Timmy, as he was the lead pony my daughters and their friends chose to ride. Timmy determined when to stop and go and the others would follow. One day a little girl fell off her pony. Her Dad asked, "What happened? Why did you fall off?" She said, "I went to sleep while riding." I guess it felt like she was being rocked to sleep.

Cowgirl Deedra on Black Cherry

Our youngest daughter, Deedra, became a cowgirl during her earliest days and a true horse lover. She was on the back of a Shetland pony as soon as she could sit and hold on and well before she was walking. She acquired skills to train them and as she grew older she transferred her love to a horse named Tonka. They had many hours of riding pleasure.

I put a sign near the rides that said "SHETLAND PONIES FOR SALE". Whenever I sold a pony, I would sell them a saddle and give them the halter free.

Half-Pint leads the way so that Alvin and Deedra
can share a pony cart ride with children visiting the zoo.

We also had a buckboard wagon (a "hug-me-tight") that I built similar to the ones in the older days that were used for courting. The front wheel cut under the front of the buggy and when you turned short, you could see how close the girl was sitting near the boy, or at least that's what I was told. This "convertible" (had no top) was all decked out and equipped with a black shiny harness and red and black upholstery. I placed plumes on top of the horses' heads for special occasions.

Half-Pint loved to be groomed and bathed. He especially enjoyed pulling the family around in a pony cart, prancing along like the greatest show horse around.

At one time, Coxville had over 100 Shetland ponies, but hunters began to shoot them while they were grazing in the fields. Apparently, this was someone's sick idea of fun. So the Coxes quit using that land except to grow oats and hay. They rented some land in Nederwald and moved the ponies back and forth to graze whenever they rotated from the barn and corrals to a pasture for grazing.

Along with this pony population, came the addition of one of the most popular attractions ever at Coxville....the Bears!

Dad told me the
BARE details ABOUT BEARS

Bears are considered to be mammals because their bodies are covered with hair and the females nurse their young with milk. They are also considered to be carnivores because they nourish their own bodies by hunting, and eating other animals.

Coxville's bear population grew to about four at one time. The zoo was even fortunate enough to have a bear cub raised in captivity. It was born blind like all cubs as its eyes didn't open until about six weeks later. Alvin always researched the animals that joined his family so that he could try to maintain their natural environment and diet even though they lived in a zoo. Each time he acquired a new animal, he would ask Doris to look it up in the World Book Encyclopedias. We learned that bears don't really hibernate because their body temperature does not drop very low.....but they sure sleep a lot during the winter months! The bear's thick coat and fat keep them warm, but they can wake up during the winter and nourish their bodies from time to time.

Since he knew that bears like to sleep in caves and dens and/or the hollow of fallen logs, he made sure that each cage he built had a "den" or "cave" and most commonly he used a concrete sewer pipe to house them.

The bears were fed a lot of chicken necks and fish from either the Coxville Lake or from avid fishermen who donated them. They also ate apples, other fruits, and the remains of dead animals which were donated to Coxville for this purpose. Examples would be when friends and customers would bring in deer that had been hit by an automobile or baby calves, goats, or lambs that died during birth on their farms.

Black bears are most common in North America and Coxville had brown bears, black bears, and a sloth bear. The brown bear is the largest land meat eater in North America so even though the ones at Coxville weren't necessarily the biggest; it still took a lot of food to fill them up.

Alvin bought one of his first bears for $200 from a man traveling through the Austin area with his bear.

Then Alvin heard there was a brown bear that someone would give him if he would pick it up in the Longview, Texas area. So he took a cage large enough to fill the bed of his pickup truck. He and Doris didn't get off to an early start because all the zoo animals had to be fed and watered before he left. After they arrived and got the bear loaded, it was indeed too late to drive back to Austin the same day. They decided to rent a "tourist court" for the night so that they could rest up before driving back the following day. Upon registration, the manager happened to see that they had a bear in a cage on the truck. He said that they couldn't stay there because of the bear. So Doris and Alvin had to go to another place that would allow "bears" to stay that night. The next morning, they discovered that their pickup truck had a flat tire that Alvin had to fix before they headed on their journey home.

Alvin also placed a very large hollowed out dead tree or wooden logs in some of his cages to make the animals feel more at home. The sloth bear seemed to appreciate this feature in his cage as they are naturally known to be good tree climbers. The sloth bears are also called "honey bears" because they like to eat honey. They also enjoy eating insects.

As the years went by Coxville acquired other bears. One that appeared to be the fiercest was a Sloth Bear, named Sam. Sam made quite a presence standing almost 6 feet tall. Sam had long fuzzy black hair and a "V" shape mark on his chest. He had very long curved white claws that looked like he could tear you apart. The claws looked similar to those you see the chiefs wear in those Cowboy & Indian movies. In the wild they are actually used to dig for ants and termites and hang from trees during the day as they are nocturnal bears. Sam was fed meat, honey, fruits and grains too. He would generally wake up as food was being served. One busy weekend morning when the zoo opened, it was discovered that some vandals had visited the zoo. Although, there was a six foot fence around the property, they still managed to find their way in. There was trash thrown about and empty liquor bottles on the ground. Alvin began to clean up the area as people entered the zoo. He soon discovered the vandals had done more than just drink that evening. They had damaged some of the locks on a few of our cages among other things. About that time, Alvin saw a crowd of people climbing the fences around the zoo and others running towards the exit. Someone said a bear was on the loose. Sam was on the move that morning. Coxville had gotten Sam from a circus that said he was fairly tame, but we had never really put it to the test. Fortunately for Alvin, the bear remembered where his groceries came from and was easily led by the collar back to his cage. Alvin found the broken lock and replaced it promptly and gave Sam some extra honey as a treat that day.

Seems like there's always one BOZO in the bunch...

Alvin bought Bozo, a black bear, from a man in Longview. He was asking $100 for him but Alvin didn't want to spend over $50 as he already had one bear. A few months later, he received a call from him saying that Alvin could have him for $50 and he was asked to ship the bear. The bear had caused him some problems so he decided to place him in a zoo. He had chosen "Coxville". Bozo was raised on a bottle during his youth and was really gentle. The owner had put a collar and chain on him, but as he grew his neck was so much bigger than his head so he had learned how to slip out of the collar.

Alvin with Bozo - January 9, 1949

First, on one of his escapades he went to the neighbor's yard and the lady was hanging up clothes. She went into the house to call the owner to come and get his bear. While she was using the phone, the little bear played havoc with the clothes and the owner had to pay the neighbor for the damage the little bear had caused.

Next he wandered a little farther from home and robbed some beehives. He wrecked the hives so the beekeeper wasn't too happy with Bozo either and was paid for the damages Bozo caused.

The last and final escape occurred when Bozo went to a nearby school. Some of the children were in the school yard eating their sack lunches and upon seeing the little bear, had scrambled into the schoolhouse leaving their lunches behind. That was when the owner decided to send Bozo packing to Coxville.

When Alvin went to pick up Bozo, the shippers were angry because they felt that the cage he had been shipped in had been too flimsy and that Bozo would be able to get out quite easily. Alvin transferred Bozo from the shipping cage to a much sturdier one by simply putting bread and apples inside the transport cage to encourage Bozo to walk right in.

Next Dad tells us about our most popular Tiger and the Lions, Too!

One of our most popular animals was our mascot Tabu, a female Bengal Tiger. Tabu was about 6 ft long with a few extra feet for her tail. She was extremely gentle and I often staked her out in the shade near the zoo entrance to welcome our visitors. You should have seen some of the faces of our visitors as they approached our entrance!

Many thought she wasn't real and sometimes she would startle a few folks. I would lead Tabu around our grounds and take her for a dip occasionally in our small lake. She seemed to especially enjoy that.

Being a Bengal Tiger, Tabu was a pure carnivore. She was fed a variety of meat; chicken necks were part of her diet. Evidently she never figured out where they came from as she had a feathered friend, a Rooster named Rufus. Often you would find him near Tabu during the day, but the funniest happened in the evening. Birds like to roost high in the trees at night, but Rufus preferred being close to his friend. Rufus would enter Tabu's enclosure and climb on top Tabu's head and roost there at night. I guess Rufus figured you couldn't ask for better protection.

In 1965, Pontiac had a "Tiger" as a symbol of the wide-tracked cars mainly because of their tiger-sized engines. Tabu, our pet tiger was used in their advertising and rode up and around Austin on top of a new Pontiac in his own big 100 foot cage. I would often take Tabu for a stroll and tell her "Come on, we're going to Austin, today." By all indications, he seemed to enjoy his outings around town.

An Air Force pilot bought a lion cub for a pet and they were quite happy until his wife was expecting a baby. They decided that one baby would be enough in their home and returned him to the zoo.

Deedra and her heavy "kitty cat"

Two university students bought pet lions. They were staying at a fraternity house and the housemother said they were cuddly and cute, but she wasn't too sure how long the boys could keep them. They only weighed 25 pounds each. The cubs slept a lot and played a lot and the students enjoyed them for a year.

It's amazing when I look back and remember just how many birds and animals were donated to our zoo. Many times though they were abandoned, injured or in poor health. In my heart and conscience, I always felt that I had done everything possible to restore them to good health or make their last days as comfortable as I could with the resources that I had available at that time.

Once when I was trying to separate a female lion from a cage with another female that had given birth to some little cubs the night before, I pushed a big transport cage into the back of my old Ford pick-up truck. An elderly man with a walking cane asked if he could watch. I said, "Yes" and got on with the job. As the lion got into the other cage, she pushed her head through a space that was a bit too large so I adjusted the space and finished loading her. But when I looked around, I noticed the walking cane was on the ground and the man was nowhere in sight. I returned to the service station and the man was inside. I asked, "Where did you go? Here's your walking cane." The man replied, "When I saw that lion put her head through that space, I thought for sure she was going to get out and my feet just wouldn't stay still!"

A "wheeler-dealer" came to the city and was planning to open a nightclub. He bought one of our lions as an attraction. She was named Cleo and the new owner planned to let the lion work with his club band. The musicians did not know of the lion's existence until he was brought in on a leash to be introduced to the members of the band. When the musicians came in to start the act and saw Cleo on a leash strolling in, three of the men dropped their instruments, tore out the door and down the street. The fourth man was too scared to run and just stood there like he couldn't move. The owner returned the lion to the zoo, which was probably a good idea since the check he had given me bounced anyway.

When I first started to remove the lion cubs from their mother for inspection and cuddling, the mother lion would pace up and down the cage and continually watch me until I returned them to her care. But in just a short time, she would learn to trust me with her most prized possessions and just lie down quite contented in her cage.   The look on her face was if to say "O.K. Alvin, you baby-sit for awhile and I'll rest some."

She seemed to sense that I would always treat them gently and return them to her unharmed.

Alvin with a pet lion

Slick, Slithering Snake Tales
As told by Alvin

There are a lot of people have "fish tales" that they like to tell over and over again......not me, I like to retell my "snake tales" and most of them are indeed true.

I acquired the snake in the picture on the next page, when one of my customers at the service station/grocery store drove in one day and said, "Here are the keys to my trunk, go see what I brought you!"   Inside that dark trunk of that car was this huge snake.   I asked where he got it. He told me that he had been living and working in New Guinea for an American company and had seen this Anaconda on the bank of the river.   He explained that the

Anaconda squeezes its prey to death if it is too big to swallow. He called to some native men to capture it, as he wanted to bring it back to Texas. After all, Texas rattlers only grow to about seven feet long. They snared the snake in, drew it tight, and one native grabbed its tail while another grabbed it in the middle. It was kind of "touch and go" for awhile, but finally they got it quieted down enough to get it in a big crate.

The customer indicated that he was coming home and had shipped the snake back because he wanted me to have it in my zoo collection. I asked in amazement, "You mean he's mine and you are donating him to the zoo?" He smiled and said "Yes, when I was a youngster and didn't have a quarter, I used to slip into the zoo by climbing a fence. This is for all the fun I had enjoying the animals!"

All of the snakes were not contained in the zoo, as there were a lot of snakes that naturally inhabited the property. Some of the native poisonous snakes in our area were the Western Diamondback Rattlesnake, the Cottonmouth Water Moccasin, Copperhead, and Coral Snakes. Most people are familiar with the saying "red and yellow" kill a fellow; red and black, friendly Jack" or red and yellow, kill a fellow; red and black, venom lack". We were taught this saying at an early age because of the area where we grew up as children and our parents knew how much we loved climbing trees, swimming in the lake or playing in the woods. Other snakes may mimic the coral snake, but a coral snake is venomous and has a blunt, black snout and bands that completely encircle their body along with yellow bands that touch the red bands and are not separated by any black or white bands. Visitors at Coxville could compare the differences of the non-venomous Milk Snake and the King Snake to the true venomous Coral snake. In all likelihood, you will not be bitten by a coral snake unless you are handling it.

Coral snakes are small, usually averaging about 24" in length but they can grow to 60". They bury themselves in the ground and leaves whenever possible. They have small fangs and since the venom takes a longer time to take effect than larger poisonous snakes, they have a tendency to hold onto the victims that they are biting. They have more potent venom than any other North American snake and their venom is 2-3 times more potent than the Western Diamondback Rattlesnake. When they are threatened, like the rattlers, they take a coil position. They bury their head under their body and their tail waves up like a fake head.

That is certainly not true of the Western Diamondback Rattlesnake. Unfortunately, we had no control over the native rattlers. As the land around us was developed into a housing development, all of the excavating and clearing of the natural habitat of these snakes was destroyed thus causing them to move into other areas. Many times we would go into the yard and see a rattler near a water faucet or a cool place. One of the interesting facts about rattlesnakes is that they don't really seek their prey; rather they find a spot where the area is abundant in prey and wait for the prey to arrive for dinner. Among their favorites are small rodents, birds, rabbits, and almost anything that can be swallowed whole. The forked tongue is used so that the snake can "taste" the air to find the prey. The diamondback also uses heat sensitive areas in the "pits" that are on the front of their heads to find their prey, even in total darkness. The Western Diamondback Rattlesnake is common in the arid Southwest United States and was certainly prevalent on our 55 acres of property outside the Austin city limits.

Another interesting fact about poisonous snakes is that their young are born alive while the non-poisonous snakes lay eggs. The new born are about 10 inches long and they continue to grow into adults of an average size of 5 feet. However, though rare, they can actually grow to 6-7 feet in length.

Rattlesnakes can swim and we had one or two occasions to actually observe this behavior viewing them from the banks of

Coxville Lake. They swim along like most other snakes except that they hold their rattlers up in order to keep them dry.

Rattlers have been collected by many people for years and one can even find them for sale in some areas at hobby and craft shows. The loud buzzing rattler sound is one that most people will not forget, especially if they have encountered it out in the wild.

Rattlesnakes are very defensive and like to guard what they consider to be their territory. Their venom attacks the blood system of whatever prey they attack.

Miss Kelley, our renter for many years raised Collie dogs and her house was next to ours. The dogs were good watchdogs and would bark and make quite a disturbance at times. When we would investigate, we would find a snake. She lost several dogs over the next few years even though they received prompt medical treatment. It just depends on what area of the dog that a snake would strike. One evening as we were getting ready to call it a day I was closing the drapes and saw a rattler asleep next to our back door. I had to keep a "22" rifle loaded for occasions like this. Another close call was late one Friday afternoon in July when my wife called to say the air conditioner was not cooling properly. July temperatures were well over 100 degrees so the house was pretty stuffy. I was thinking I would need to add Freon so I took my tools and threw them on top of the air conditioning unit and got down to remove the back cover. I called to my wife to ask if she heard a rattling noise thinking it was coming from the unit. She cried "Hurry Alvin, get away...there's a snake on top of the unit." It had been covered with some brown leaves as it was near a hedge and was coiled and ready to strike. If he had hit me, it would have been directly in the face.

Rattlesnakes come in a range of colors such as gray, tan, and black and sometimes a yellowish, red, or green coloration. A more rare color is the albino which lacks the protective camouflage of the other rattlers.

A customer came in one day and said "Cox, you need some snakes! Not many people see different varieties of snakes." Just a short time later, an African American neighbor came in the store and said "I have a big white rattlesnake in my outhouse." I said, "If you bring him in I'll buy it." He said, "Oh no, you come get him, he's yours free!" So I went to the man's home and there was a big Albino rattlesnake. I got a cane-fishing pole, took some string and made a loop to snare and lift the snake with. I sacked him up and put him in a big fish aquarium to be displayed and fed him mice and eggs. Not many people had ever seen an Albino rattlesnake before. A short time later a dairyman said he found another Albino rattlesnake so I took off to snare it. He had the snake under a five-gallon bucket with a large rock on top to secure it. I took a piece of tin and slid it under the bucket and was a little disappointed because it was just about 18 inches long and only had one rattler and a button. I placed the two together and much to my surprise the young snake was a male and the larger one a female. It was ironic that apparently I had been given a pair.   That year, the female had four babies, but they were born prematurely and didn't live very long. The next litter consisted of ten babies. They were born alive in a sac and coiled up and ready to strike. When I retired, I had sixteen albino rattlesnakes when I sold them to a collector in Houston, Texas for $1,000.

I have a story about a "hitchhiking snake". Seems a man called and asked if I would come and get a big snake out of his flowerbed. This neighbor had been on a visit to the valley and he saw this snake crawl out from underneath the neighbor's car. It was a nice Blue Indigo.

We also had a Blue Indigo snake, which was quite large, and little boys would like to hold him. He would wrap himself around them and they could put on quite a show of bravery. The expressions on their faces were truly something to see.

Once I took a big Anaconda or water boa to show the television audience on the "Uncle Jay Show". That particular snake weighed over seventy pounds and was thirteen and a half feet long. I took two men with me to help carry the snake as he was more than a handful when he wiggled and squirmed about.

Bertha's Personal Copperhead Experience

My mother, Bertha Cox, went to the parrot house about dusk one evening to check on the parrots' water. As she was about to enter the back of the parrot house, she felt something sting her ankle, then another and another. It was a large copperhead and he was by the water faucet. She was 78 years old then and we packed her foot in ice and took her to the hospital. She was in a lot of pain and her foot was pretty swollen when we arrived but she recovered after several months of dealing with a bad leg.

Copperheads bite more people in most years than other U.S. species of snakes but they have the mildest venom. Their initial threat is to strike while other snakes will try to escape from humans if they have enough warning. Rattlers will commonly vibrate their tails and cottonmouths will sit with their mouths open as a warning. Copperheads seldom inject much venom with their bites.

Another poisonous snake that I kept at Coxville on display was the Cottonmouth Water Moccasin. This snake is the only poisonous water snake in North American and is an aggressive reptile that will stand its ground and sometimes even approach the intruder. They average 30 inches in length but can grow to 54 inches in some areas. They like to lay dormant on tree branches and rocks around areas of water. The adults usually have brown, black or olive bodies with lighter bellies. The young are born alive and are similar in color to the Copperhead snakes. Copperheads like other poisonous snakes have heads that are triangular in shape because they store poison in their glands. Poisonous snakes also have slitted and not rounded eyes. Snakes smell with their tongues because they have poor eyesight. They feel vibrations to sense their surroundings so it never hurts to walk heavy if you are walking at night in order to give the snake adequate warning to retreat.

Snake Bite Treatment

I cannot help but include a little bit about the precautions and the things I learned while housing these critters. Hopefully, neither you nor anyone you know will encounter this experience firsthand. The best protection against snake bites is prevention. Avoid tall grassy areas and be cautious where you place your hands and feet.

During the years of Coxville, a lot of people carried snake bite kits which contained a knife, two rubber suction cups and a tourniquet. The object was to cut an "X" in the victim's skin over each fang puncture. The person treating the bite used their mouth to suction out the injected venom. The tourniquet was placed between the wound and the heart in an attempt to reduce the venom from traveling into the blood stream. In some cases, this treatment left ugly scars and in the worst cases, the loss of the affected limb as the venom mimics a meat tenderizer.

Later updated medical studies made advances in treatment. Newer methods of treating snake bites suggest that the affected area be removed, allowing the wound to heal. Involved parties are advised to dial "911" and if at all possible, identify the snake involved in the attack. The next action after calling for emergency assistance should be to wash the bite if possible with soap and water, immobilize the bite area, and cover the area with ice. It is very important to keep that area lower than the heart. It is best to cover the area with a clean, cool compress to minimize the swelling. It is a good idea to remove the victim's jewelry such as rings and watches as there may be a lot of swelling. Some of the common symptoms to look for after an individual has been bitten are fang marks and swelling at the site of the bite, bloody wound discharge, and localized pain. The victim could be in shock, in an altered mental state, and/or having breathing difficulties. The victim may understandably feel weak, dizzy, have excessive sweating, and blurred vision. They may be nauseated and experience vomiting, loss of muscle coordination, rapid pulse, and diarrhea.

Severity of the poisonous snake bite depends on the type and size of the snake and how much venom it injected (if any at all) and the potency. Sometimes the bites are actually "dry bites" and 35% of bites are mild. The odds are in the victims' favor as only 10-15% is usually severe. Other factors that need to be determined are the location of where they occurred on the body and the depth of bite(s). Other important information would include the general health of the person who was bitten, their physical size and age.

Nonpoisonous snakes can cause infections and allergic reactions to some people. Only about 5% of snakes found in the United States are actually poisonous; however there can also be health problems caused by nonpoisonous snakes such as boa constrictors, pythons or anacondas. Pressure applied by these large snakes can affect the victim's bones, joints, and muscles.

Alvin talks about his
Feathered Friends ...

The mynah birds were quite an attraction and very good talkers. It seemed that they would latch on to a new word most every week, sometimes rather naughty. One Sunday, a lady with shorts stopped by and upon entering the "Ladies Room" heard this piercing wolf-whistle. She went into the grocery part of the store and asked "Where is the man that whistled at me in the restroom?" My mother said, "That wasn't a man that was Jimmy, our mynah bird." I don't think she was convinced that was the truth until fortunately Jimmy let out another whistle and said, "What's your name?"

After she left, my Mother said, "I think she was a little disappointed that it wasn't a man!"

A small boy of about 5 years old was looking at the birds one day when our bird named Jimmy said "Hello, Jimmy" to a little boy. The child turned to his Mom with total disbelief of how that bird knew his name.

I had a neighbor with an old two-story home that had owls in the attic. Owls can be very helpful as they eat rats but my neighbor wanted to rid his home of the owls. I went up into the attic and discovered a nest full of baby owls too young to feed on their own so I decided they had a better chance of survival if I left them a couple of weeks. When I returned to get them, I brought them to the zoo and placed them in an aviary with a tall roof that had a place for them to hide in the top away from the crowds of people. I fed them mice and chicken necks. They were so comical when they saw their food and would turn their heads all around from side-to-side before eating their prey. As they young owls matured, they had a nest in the top of the aviary and one by one the new little ones would come down, so fuzzy and cute.

One duck in the zoo had everyone baffled. I thought it was a "Wood Duck" but the Texas Game Commission didn't think it was and was unable to identify what kind it was. We called him "No Name Duck".

I bought six yellow-head parrots in Waco and placed them in a home next to the mynah birds thinking they might acquire some language skills when they heard the mynah birds talking. Not so, they just squawked and whistled, but not one word did they ever utter. Then I rented some monkeys and these parrots to a man that was opening his fruit stand. When he returned them to me they still did not talk. Then one day I decided to move the parrots to another cage and caught them in a net. When I put the net over one he hollered "Help" followed by "Hello, Polly". That was the beginning of their vocabulary.

I had a white Cockatoo named "Waldo". As a favor, a man asked me to keep him one day until he could work it out with his wife to let the bird stay in their home. One day he got loose and flew on top of the service station and then high onto the power lines across the busy highway. He held on by his claws, trying to reach the other wire. I was pretty upset since it wasn't even my bird and began to envision "fried bird". After an hour or so of freedom, the bird decided to return to me. I approached him with an apple and then threw a net over him as he said "bye bye".

A neighbor from Waters Park had a big pond and called one day to see if I had a pelican missing from the zoo. I told him I had never had one so he asked if I would like to come over and see if I could catch it as it had been standing near the water for quite some time. I think that he got lost from his companions maybe in flight because we had some stormy weather just before he was found. He was really exhausted and hungry so it's wasn't hard for me to coax him with a fish. I took him to the zoo that had a water pool inside and all fenced even on top of the pen so nothing could get him. He kept me busy trying to supply him with the little fish from our private lake. One day I was pushing a feed cart though the zoo to feed the meat eating animals some chicken necks. The pelican had become very gentle and I decided to let him out to roam free around the zoo. When I turned around after feeding other animals, I saw him dipping in the cart and scooping up a pouch full of chicken. He would swallow a few and then come back for more. After that, if I didn't have enough fish, he would finish off his meals with chicken necks for dessert.

Soon after that I got another Pelican. Someone had found it beside the road and discovered that his eye had been shot out with BBs. He was very weak and hungry so I took on another boarder. The two seemed to get along just fine and lived to be quite old birds, amusing all age groups who watched them at the zoo.

I had an assortment of fowl and birds and noticed that sometimes the hens would not set on their eggs. I got a big Wyandotte hen from a friend to set on pheasant, quail, turkey, peacock, guineas, Chinese silkies or whatever I needed to hatch. She was in the pen with all of these other fowl and sometimes would steal a nest of her own choosing to hatch. We still had more eggs than this mama hen could take care of so we purchased an incubator.

A candy retailer had some stale candy and asked if we could use it to feed any of the animals. We had bears and monkey that were fond of candy and thought they really had a special treat.

I took several cases to the lake house where my parents were living at that time and placed it on the covered-screened porch. There were geese on the lake in front of the house and they would come to the area close to the backyard fence where my Mother was raising Pekinese and Chihuahua dogs at the time.   There were raccoons, opossums, skunks and other varmints that were disturbing the geese at nesting time. One mother goose decided that if she built her nest close to the barking dogs, she would be safe so she got on the porch were the candy was stored to keep it cool. One night she pecked holes in the candy boxes and lined her nest with candy bars, paper and all. However, later only two little goslings were able to hatch because most of the eggs were covered with way too much sticky chocolate.

With Thanks to Our Special Employees

Lee Zertuche, Mexican-American, was a friendly polite employee that worked for Coxville during Alvin's first ten years in business. He was very dependable and a dedicated worker.

Wylie Ochoa, another Mexican-American, started as a young teenager and worked until he was about eighteen.

Two other young Mexican-Americans worked for a number of years helping train the horses and working the pony rides.

Another young man started his first job with us and stayed until he was about eighteen. He later continued his education and is now and has been for years, a Baptist minister. He was living in the hill country, but when Manford Cox died, we all wanted Allen Cearley to give the memorial service at his funeral.

Allen Cearley's brother, Victor, was another dedicated worker. We thought that Victor would be single all of his life, but as he got more mature, probably in his thirties, he married and made a good family man. These young men came from a good Christian family, Charles and Edna Cearley, so it was no surprise to us that they made good citizens.

"Interesting" Customers

As told by Doris

You can't be in business for almost 50 years without having some humorous and bad experiences with all the people you come in contact with from all walks of life. There was a large, buxom woman who came into the store almost weekly and I suspected that she was stealing from me but I never could catch her in the act. One day I planned to outsmart her. While I was slicing her a pound of cheese and some lunchmeat with my back turned, I glanced into a small mirror that I had installed and saw that she was placing a package of Lance's fried pies down her bosom. When I totaled her bill, I said, "I will be glad to add the pies you have to your bill." She said "No sir, I didn't get any pies". When I asked about the ones that she had hidden in her blouse, she denied it so I started around the counter and said, "I'll just get them out." Boy did she start removing pies then and placed five pies on the counter. She returned to buy groceries from me at the store many times after that but each and every time she would always say "Mr. Cox, I promise I ain't gonna steal no more from you.....and she didn't!

One day a lady arrived and wanted to buy a pony. The well-dressed lady was especially persistent in bargaining for a lower price.

After we came to terms, she asked if I thought she could carry the pony in her automobile. I walked out to see how much room she had back of the seat and noted that it was a roomy Cadillac driven by a chauffeur. I told her I would get an old blanket to put in the back seat. She said "Don't worry, this is my old car and the chauffeur replied "she has a new Cadillac at home". I just thought to myself, "Wouldn't you just know that this is the customer who tried to get me to reduce the price of the pony".

I provided service on one of my old neighbor's cars. He told me about his first Model T he had owned. Apparently he and his brother were driving home from Austin one day and noticed it was not running very good. The brother thought that it probably needed a quart of oil so they bought some. However, they couldn't find where to put the oil in as they had always had someone to care for their car. The brother suggested that they just pour the oil over the motor as that might help some and they did just that. However, it smoked so badly, they hardly made it home.

Another couple, Mr. and Mrs. Adams lived about a mile back of our property and store. Since they didn't own a car, Mr. Adams bought most of his groceries from Coxville. He walked with a "tow sack" carried over his shoulders. (A tow sack or potato sack found many uses in farm homes and was a good and practical way to carry a load.) Their sons took care of picking up their other needs by car.

Doris recalls that perhaps the best part of the business for her was some of the customers. She had never been associated with the Swedish or African American cultures when she grew up around Guadalupe County around Fentress and Staples, Texas. She felt she understood the Mexican people because she taught their children. She loved Mexican food and knew they strived to please their employers. However, Doris was really surprised by the Swedish people's contagious sense of humor.

Darlene and Aunt Fannie

One of my favorite customers was a very wise and witty woman that everyone called "Aunt Fannie". She had a son named L. G. Hancock. Everyone around Waters Park and far North Austin knew and respected this family. She was so excited when after our years of marriage; my wife delivered our first child, a daughter that we named Darlene on July 25, 1945.

When she came to call, my wife told her that our baby had colic. Aunt Fannie said "My goodness, I know what will help her!" She returned in a few days with a necklace that had an asafetida ball on it and said to put it around Darlene's neck. It wasn't a "sure cure" but it was certainly worth a try!

Sometimes I would often return a favor to Aunt Fannie by sending her an opossum and would toss in some sweet potatoes. Once, I made a mistake and failed to send sweet potatoes. She sent word that the opossum was sure good but that I had forgotten to send her any sweet potatoes. I was careful not to make that mistake again.

"Aunt Fannie" lived to be over one hundred years old. On her 100th birthday, friends and neighbors from all around came to help her celebrate her big day.

On that special day she requested that one of the farmers let her pick cotton from his field, just to see if she could still do it. He told her to go ahead and give it a try and they took pictures of her while she picked away!

"Longhorns Return" as told by Alvin

In 1972, my health was not what it needed to be and I was hospitalized and not able to work in the store for several months. At that time, the zoo was already closed and it was difficult to find help to keep the grocery store and service station open as it had been 7 days a week, 24 hours a day, so we closed at nights. We had a big set of Longhorns over the outside door entrance. One morning when I returned to the store to open up for the day, I noticed that the horns were missing. Those horns had been with me for a long, long time and I was really disappointed that someone would steal them.

In 1983, about eleven years later, a young man drove into the service station and said he needed some gas to get home. I told him that we couldn't sell on credit. He then said, "Do you remember that set of longhorns that you had hanging over your store's entrance? Well, I stole them and I'll return them when I come back to pay you for the gas." My Dad, Manford Cox, said he couldn't believe that I would give gasoline to a man that had admitted he had stolen my horns. I have to admit that I didn't expect to ever see those horns again and knew I had taken a pretty big gamble on this customer. Well this man did return the horns to me the very next day and explained that he and a couple of buddies had been drinking beer and drove through the station when it was closed and decided to take the horns. He said that it had been on his conscience ever since. He never did tell me his name and I never asked.

COXVILLE IN THE NEWS

(All of the following articles appeared on various dates in American Statesman newspapers.)

To the best of our records, Coxville first appeared in the American Statesman newspaper on March 17, 1946 because of this shamrock of its resemblance to the St. Patrick's emblem.

This unusual rock was a favorite when viewed by many people. Peter Organ found this rock that looked like a big shamrock. At the entrance of the rock garden was this centerpiece for the large gold fish pond that was built with some of the rarest rocks. The Cactus and Rock Garden featured a train that ran through a unique village made of different types of rock.

In the <u>American-Statesman</u>, Sunday edition on July 25, 1948, the following was written: "Mrs. Cox's hobby has grown rather expensive since she now has rocks from each state in America and almost every country in the world. Rocks from the states were mailed to her, and those from the various countries were brought back by tourists. Petrified logs, weighing twice as much as regular rocks, have been hauled to Coxville from all over Texas. They are now displayed in an area surrounding the Cox's curio shop which was closed during the war.

A rock menagerie of natural formations include the three bears, a watermelon patch, dogs, goats, rabbits, a cat, fish, a mermaid, the devil, turtles, kangaroos, lions, the old woman on the hill, birds, and an Indian campfire scene. Shamrock and cave formations are other drawing cards in the rock garden. Fossils and cactus plants surround the Coxville fish pond."

Children are always interested in the miniature farm house and chicken shack of rock. They are surrounded by a model train, highways, busses, trucks, and trailer parks.

"Colorful Coxville Zoo Developed From Hobby".
July 25, 1948

Seven pictures were featured and though they quality is difficult to reprint, the text was as follows:

ANIMAL KINGDOM – Showtime at Coxville brings out citizens of A. W. Cox's animal kingdom. Caught in their respective quarters at the private zoo, four miles from the city limits on Dallas Highway are:

An alert deer, with horns in the velvet stage of development, and his grazing friend...a strutting male peacock displaying his richly colored tail feathers to an appreciative hen...a dead-serious javelin thinking over some world-shattering problem in the hog world with her young offspring...two graceful white herons gaze hopefully across the cool expanse of Coxville's fish stocked lake...A. W. Cox clamps a cigar firmly in his mouth while his father, M. J. Cox adjusts a restraining strap on "Christine Churchill" , a playful pet monkey...a hungry pelican looks eagerly for another handout like his recent 45-fish dinner ... "chow down" for the kingdom's reigning monarch, a 250 pound Mexican lion...a stiff tailed monkey wistfully hugs the enclosing wire of his cage and thinks of the peanut-filled world outside.

Stableford Cars Sport Real Tiger

Jack Stableford Pontiac, 1014 Lamar Boulevard, has stationed a 200-pound tiger atop one of his 1965 Pontiacs as a less than subtle reminder that the General Motors cars have a tiger-like engine under the hood.

"Tabu" will be riding in a Stableford Pontiac for about a week, according to a company spokesman.

The orange and white animal has become the symbol of the wide-tracked cars mainly because of their tiger-size engines of 421 cubic inches in the Pontiac 2-plus-2 and the 389 cubic inch engine in the Le Mans GTO.

Like Tigers, Pontiacs are quick, agile, and furious, lithe, lean and nimble.

Pontiac tigers run better on gasoline than "cat food", a spokesman quickly added.

Another newspaper article written by Jack Guinn was titled:

Every Day is Circus Day at Coxville Gardens

Near City Where Proprietor Has Everything

From Rocks to Monkeys on Display

Coxville Gardens are located eight miles north of Austin on the Dallas highway. They were started in 1936 with a rock that looked like a kitten, and now consist of driveways and walks lined with odd-looking rock, from every state in the union and five foreign countries.

Most is Given*: Mrs. Cox buys a lot of the rock, but most of it is given to her, she said. The rocks from the various states were sent to her by people who stopped at the filling station and remembered to send something back when they got home.*

She has one rock from Belgium, given her by a little boy who brought his collection of rocks with him when his family fled from Nazi invasion. Others are from France, Germany, Great Britain, and Puerto Rico. A school teacher in Puerto Rico, who had attended the University of Texas, sent in the Puerto Rican item.

Prize Collection*: Mrs. Cox' prize collection is a shamrock, plowed up by a Negro named Peter Organ, who donated it to the garden. In the center of the garden, which is rapidly spreading out in all directions, is a sort of panorama of civilization depicting in miniature. This was started in 1936 and had been intended to symbolize Texas centennial celebration.*

Houses, barns, churches, railway stations involved in this miniature civilization were modeled by Mrs. Cox out of concrete.

Made in a rough cone-shape about 15 feet across at the base, the Coxville version of Texas civilization begins and ends in violence. The beginning shows toy pioneers battling Indians, and the end, which is the present day, presumably depicts man's one-sided conflict with motorized transportation – a miniature automobile smashed into the side of a miniature mountain. The circular story in toys goes from a covered wagon to an electric, stream-lined train.

Sole protection of the collection is a little sign stuck in the dirt which says "Thou Shalt Not Steal."

Collection Varies*: Mrs. Cox' collection of rocks varies from petrified trees to chunks of shale which have fallen apart in the form of animals. Clearly identified are rabbits, giraffes, ducks, and cows. Three large boulders look like three bears and two others placed nose to nose are referred to by Mrs. Cox as the gingham dog and the calico cat. She says her most appreciative visitors are children.*

Lion Comes Home
Author Unknown

That lion is back again. The Coxville zoo lion that customarily spends a few months in South Texas with its owner is back in its familiar cage at the Dallas highway zoo and rock garden. Also back after the annual "vacation" are two bobcats and several pair of javelin hogs.

The Grocery Bill

In 1948, Alvin told newspaper reporters that his pelican had a good appetite and could eat 45 fish at one meal. He said that the bird was brought to him after it was found shot on the highway.

A green-legged heron also came to him via the finder method. It was discovered on East Avenue.

An annual fee of $5 was required to keep a license for his fur bearing animals. Alvin stated that you would not find any "Don't Feed the Animals' sign at Coxville. He just asked that visitors remember not to feed their hands to the animals as well! Donation cans were placed at the entrance to the free zoo and contributed only $12 of the $32 required weekly to feed the animals back then.

Each week, two barrels of bread and a $12.50 supply of horse and mule feed along with hen scratch was on Cox's grocery list. Horse meat figured at $5 weekly at 20 cents a pound. Chicken necks added up to 36 gallons at a quarter per gallon.

We had good sources of food to feed the animals, otherwise we would not have been able to feed and take care of them properly. A local chicken restaurant named The Chicken Shack sold us gallons of chicken necks and scraps for a quarter a gallon. Chicken necks were the staple diet of many of the animals. Every day the lions and hyenas ate between 60-70 chicken necks. The three bobcats ate a dozen each; the two red foxes had six each; the three gray foxes had four each; the five skunks had two each; and various amounts were eaten by all the other animals, excepting animals such as monkeys and deer.

We obtained large quantities of day old bread and horse and chicken feed in one hundred pound sacks. Bananas, other fruit and vegetables that were not top quality but still good for animals, were obtained at reasonable prices. Alvin also located peanuts, cookies, and honey for the bears. He had many friends in the community and often they would help donate scraps or extra quantities of food for the animals to enjoy.

An estimate of food for the 500 animals, birds, and reptiles in 1949 was as follows:

- 374 pounds of meat
- 2 barrels of bread
- 100 pounds of horse and mule feed
- 224 bananas

- 100 pounds of hen scratch
- plus a variety of grapes, peanuts, cakes, cookies, honey (for the bears), and many other things.

Another article appeared with the photo shown below:

Coxville Zoo Has 500 Wild Animals
By Bill Brammer
April 15, 1954

If you'd like to get back to nature, snuggle right up to it, in fact the Coxville Zoo should give you an outlet. The animal empire 4 miles out on the Dallas Highway has just about everything that leaps, crawls, roars and writhes-from coyotes, to crows from black bears to lions and pelicans and alligators.

There are more than 500 animals; some eat horse meat, some eat flowers and seed and some eat each other. Many in fact eat people.

You won't find any "Don't Feed the Animals" signs either. They are always hungry and owner A. W. Cox requests that only visitors don't feed them a finger, or a hand, or an arm.

The sprawling 55 acre zoo is deceiving. Fronting on the Dallas highway, you see only a few monkey cages, a service station, and a grocery store.

But when you pay your quarter, there's a thrill in every cage. There are hundreds of cages, too. The trails twist and wind far back into the wooded areas as far back as Cox's artificial lake, already stocked with fish and waiting only for a shipment of herons and pelicans and other water-birds.

Coyotes burrow underground, alligators sun themselves in their private pool, the black bears argue with each other and thirteen "midget" Shetland ponies romp in their pen.

There are deer - a buck, a stag, and a doe - and raccoons and foxes and pelicans and peacocks. There are timber wolves and dogs, pole cats and civet cats and ringtail cats along with dead-serious javelinas and mean, lean hyenas.

There is a sweet old lion named Cheetah and several other lions that'll eat your hand and anything else that's offered.

There are monkeys - 25 of them - and white mice and lovebirds and turtles and foxes, and pumas and pheasants and lizards and snakes of several select varieties.

Right now, Cox is building a bigger and better lion cage. Then he hopes to put Cheetah in with some of the meaner males, "may soften them up a little. And if we get some lion cubs, I figure I might be able to trade them off for a leopard. We don't have a leopard."

It was surprising to find something Cox does not have: like leopards and rhinoceros and elephants and sperm whales. He has just about everything else.

It all started in 1939 when he bought a monkey. He bought another, then another; then he began collecting other specimens. "After you get enough of them, people hear about you and start giving you things."

"Soldiers, sailors, and marines brought home many of these animals after the war. And in many cases, it was either the monkey or the wife so I have acquired many would-be home breakers".

Mrs. Cox protested at first, but now she's becoming adjusted to how the coyotes and the lions roar late at night. "Its out-of-hand now", she said. "There is no telling, how many animals, what with white mice and guinea pigs, and parrots and rabbits."

The problem there is feeding the animals, horsemeat and chicken necks and mule feed and live fish are usually on the menu. Two barrels of bread per week is not unusual. "It's a full time job for me, my wife, and the zookeeper," said the animal's impresario, "but look at the friends we have".

That's How It Bounces

Did Wade Hampton write one hot check to buy a night club and then write another hot check to buy a lion to attract customers?

Well, said Hampton, now in county jail on two other indictments, the answer is yes and no.

The 26-year-old real estate salesman admits he became the proprietor of the Avalon Club, 6200 North Lamar, under somewhat confusing circumstances, and that he became temporary owner of the six-month-old Coxville lion cub Cleopatra under embarrassing circumstances. But, said he, sitting in the jail visiting room, let me explain and so he did:

Late in May he developed a yearning to buy the Avalon and he flew to Dallas to dicker with the man who he thought owned the place.

The supposed owner wanted $808.50 for the club and Wade wrote a check.

I had that much in my pocket, but not in the bank, Wade said. Of course, I meant to put it in the bank, but then I found out this guy didn't really own the club, so I just let his check bounce.

Not only did he discover he was just a renter, not an owner, says Hampton, but he found that the rent was due and the atmosphere in need of some jazzing up.

So he jazzed. He hired a four piece colored dance band and he sent his assistant out to Coxville Zoo to buy Cleopatra-with a rubber check. All went well for a time. Business boomed. Cleopatra ate her two cans of dog food and one large can of sardines each day and grew fat.

Then the decline came. Up to this time, Cleopatra had been used to attract customers during the day and the dance band at night. The musicians did not know of Cleo's existence until the night that Hampton planned for band and lion to work together.

Those boys came in here and saw Cleopatra and dropped their instruments and just tore out the door and down the street, Hampton recalled wistfully. That is, three of them did. The fourth just stood there. Too scared to run, I guess. Anyway, the band refused to work with Cleo, so I am sending her back.

And none too soon, complains the Coxville Zoo, which now had discovered the purchased check was not good.

Wade's wife, Peggy, who had become attracted to Cleo, took her pet back to Coxville on Friday afternoon. Wade had closed the Avalon the night before.

And there are one or two other checks yet to be explained.

Austin's new Barnum has fallen on evil days.

Another article appearing on Monday, July 14, 1980 was about the tourist courts in the Austin area and featured Coxville Courts and Zoo as part of that article. It read:

"I had three cottages I built in 1939," said A. W. Cox, 64. I rented the rooms for $1.50 a night, but by the time I closed them, they were up to $4.50.

Cox had a service station and grocery, which he still operates, as well as a 50 cents-a-day fishing hole and the zoo, which grew from the acquisition of one monkey in 1939.

But when the interstate opened, Cox's gas sales dropped from 21,000 gallons a month to 3,000 gallons, and the cottage trade plummeted. In 1969, he closed the zoo.

An article titled **"Marilyn Does, but She Doesn't"** appeared on April 14, 1954 and read as follows:

Marilyn is a beauteous monkey residing at Coxville Zoo who has been snubbed by the young swains of late. Marilyn wanted to be a mother, but the boys wouldn't cooperate. Out of desperation, she "adopted" a passing rat Sunday, and she hasn't let go yet.

Marilyn, a sweet young thing Coxville Zoo is feeling the real mother instinct these days. Marilyn is a pigtail monkey who figured last week that the various young swains who abound in and about Coxville hadn't done right by her. She was at that age, you know, and it was spring. Trouble was, the boys have been bashful, downright snobbish, in fact.

"I say this in all modesty", said Marilyn modestly. I am not unattractive. These goons just don't know a good monkey when they see one."

Marilyn wants to settle down, like all sweet young girls, and raise a family. A cage with a white picket fence and the little ones swinging through the treetops sound enchanting. Gerald, a spider monkey who lives just around the corner would be just the ticket as a mate and pappy-monkey, but Gerald isn't interested.

So mate less Marilyn, with the exalted look of young motherhood, reached her last recourse this week and took advantage of it.

A rat, and not a very pretty one, strolled into Marilyn's cage Sunday and found the sweetest mammy in the world waiting for him.

Marilyn grabbed the rat and hasn't let go yet.

Perhaps she mistook the peacocks, or geese, or buzzards nearby for the stork. A. W. Cox, impresario of the animal empire on the Dallas Highway, isn't sure.

At any rate, Marilyn has a family now and she's never been happier. She hasn't rolled those big brown eyes at Gerald or any other monkey in days.

She was still hugging the rat Wednesday, cooing and singing and making mother talk.

"It's the sweetest thing," said Marilyn. "I changed its formula and now it hardly ever cries".

She admits that colic was a problem for a while and those 2 am feedings were exhausting.

"This is all I wanted. I can get by," said Marilyn. "What more would any girl ask?"

Marilyn hasn't released her loving mother's grip on the weary rat since Sunday. She's gentle, but Cox is wondering if the rat is getting hungry.

The rat hasn't said a word, and neither have the other mother monkeys. Gerald, spokesman for the males, said: "She's psychotic, who wants to marry a complex?"

Marilyn, nevertheless, has adjusted. Whether or not the rat adjusts remains to be seen.

• •

These news stories document the exceptional existence of Coxville and the man who loved it with all his heart.

His family could hear the sounds of change and feel the rapid pace at which it was surrounding this beloved man and his precious animals.

As his daughter, I knew the pain he would feel when he had to close this chapter of his life; that he so cherished.

• •

With Time.....Things Change

There was never a charge to visit Coxville Rock Garden. In return, all the family asked was that the public not deface it. Unfortunately, there are always a few who ruin it for all the others. It seems that those few just couldn't resist "taking a souvenir". Vandals started to take what they wanted even though most of the items were cemented in place. A boy was trying to get a doll from the dollhouse for his girlfriend, broke a glass window and left with a bloody arm after he broke off the doll's head. The rock garden began to show its toll and eventually was closed.

The dam and the lake are no longer there, as the property sold and became a new park, Walnut Creek Metropolitan Park, in North Austin. During the city's process of developing ballparks, the dam was destroyed so there was very little water left in the creek. All along the bank of this creek there was an area with rocky ledges and a lot of fossil formations and large animal footprints (some of which were very large and unusual). After this property sold, no one realized what was in this area, and the fossils were covered with tons of dirt and rocks. Children used to play there, and it was very easy for them to imagine some prehistoric creature coming to the water hole. Their imaginations were very vivid or were they?

As the Cox family looks back, they can "chuckle" at some, but certainly not all of the problems that had really distressed them at times. One rumor got out that Coxville was feeding puppies to the lions. These little puppies were only held in cages as temporary homes until they could be adopted by good families. However, one time the rumor got all the way to the County Sheriff's office causing them to come out and investigate. The party who filed the complaint came along with the Sheriff. He was finally able to note upon closer observation that the food being fed to the lions had hooves on it. Pointing out that dogs don't have hooves, he felt pretty foolish. Alvin was contacted quite often by the dairies whenever a new born baby calf would die at birth and was called to come and pick them up for animal food. He would pay a couple of dollars to the hired man who would help him load it.

Another story involved a report that a baboon was infested with ticks. We had never had a tick problem with our animals and most people who have ever observed monkeys noted that they are constantly picking at themselves. The baboon did have small warts on his face.

Memories Live On

Time changes our lives... sometimes for the better... sometimes not, but nonetheless changes are inevitable and must be made. The city of Austin grew and grew and soon Coxville was no longer outside the city limits. A new housing development soon bordered the Coxville property. Not all the neighbors were excited about their yards being bordered by "wild" animals.

Alvin Cox loved his animals with all his heart. He derived a lot of pleasure and satisfaction knowing thousands were able to enjoy these animals. However, it was becoming more and more difficult for him to care for his pets both physically and financially.

In 1969, Alvin had spent over thirty years, training, petting, loving, and providing housing and dinner for his pets at Coxville. It was time to retire. But his dedication continued as he found new homes for his animals with individuals in Travis County. Other animals went to Dallas, Abilene and Houston zoos.

He nursed many an animal and had a special gift of relating to their souls. He will long be remembered by thousands of people, both young and old, who enjoyed his animals.

Years later, Alvin moved this rock, the petrified wood and other rocks to his home in Round Rock, Texas. He built another goldfish pond around it to enjoy during his retirement years. After his death some rock favorites including the shamrock and the rocks resembling a bear and cat were moved once again to Denison, Texas where they continue to be enjoyed by family and friends over seventy years later and keep Mary Ruth's memory alive.

I remember visiting the rock garden as I grew up at Coxville and it was always one of my very favorite places to be. I never saw another place that was anything like it and I could imagine how happy Mary Ruth would have been to have played in it if she had just lived a few more years. It was an attraction that I was proud to show my friends whenever they came over and I would go there to listen to the giggles and squeals of laughter by others touring it for the first time.   Sometimes.....I think I could actually feel Mary Ruth's presence.

Doris Cox wrote to her three daughters...

This is our personal history of
many happy memories and some trials
along the way and how it came to be,
"Coxville", a hobby that grew by "leaps and bounds".
After retirement, my husband would
recall these stories and relive them.
Our sons-in-law heard them over and over again
and would remark,
"Each time I hear Alvin's stories, I learn something new".
The "girls" wanted a book as there were many
things they were too young to remember.
Thanks Norman, for all your support.
Chris, our only grandchild, remember your Grandpa!
To each of you, my love.
I am so fortunate to have such a loving family.

Doris Hunsucker Cox – 2008

Clearly, one of the main reasons for Alvin's success was the woman who worked by his side year after year and helped him follow his dreams. Alvin had some pretty "crazy" ideas sometimes and she provided the balance that made him successful. She "put up with" lots of animals in the house which obviously means a lot of "clean-up". She made healthy homemade meals for him, his parents and the three daughters. She made the girls' clothes, she did all the bookkeeping, she was active in PTA, Girl Scouts, 4-H, and the girls' school activities. Not only was she a remarkable mother, but she was always his partner and willing to go on all his adventures in life.

Doris Cox retired to Sherman, Texas and is a "Super Senior". At 89 years of age, she is in good health and remains very active. She lives within miles of her daughter, Denise and her son-in-law, Norman. Chris, her only grandson, lives in Evanston, Illinois. Darlene Cox Davis lives with her husband, Jim in Oklahoma. The youngest daughter, Deedra Cox Thompson and her husband, Russ live in West Palm Beach.

Doris is an excellent cook and specializes in fried chicken, homemade dressing, and lemon meringue pie. She is an avid gardener and enjoys raising bluebirds. Doris is active in her church, participates in exercise classes, and enjoys playing cards with friends. Doris continued her love for Chihuahuas with pets Tootsie, Wrinkles, and later Chica who lived until Doris' 87th birthday.

Mom and Me

About the Author

I would never describe myself as an author and I never intend to write another book as I have struggled with this one over the years...however, I did have a story that needed to be told and it needed to be told "by family". There is another reason, I wrote this.....and that was to fulfill a promise to my Mother.

I was born as the middle daughter of Alvin and Doris Cox. I enjoyed a normal childhood, but had the extra advantage of being a zookeeper's child who had endless playmates including ponies, lion cubs and baby fawns.

In 1972, Norman Robinson asked for my hand in marriage and I readily accepted, before he changed his mind. We moved to Spokane, Washington in 1977 with a beautiful baby boy named Chris. In 1983, our family moved to Taipei, Taiwan for the better part of three years, as Norman was General Manager of a keyboard manufacturing facility.

In addition to seeing that part of our world, we were fortunate to travel to Korea, Australia, Japan, New Zealand, Hong Kong, Mexico, Canada, Germany, Italy, France, Belgium, England, Switzerland, and most of the United States.

My favorite pastimes are fishing, photography, bird watching, growing flowers, traveling, reading, and shopping. Most importantly, I enjoy spending time with friends and family which includes our Dalmatian, Yahtzee. Our only son, Chris, lives in Evanston, Illinois and plans to marry the 'girl of his dreams" in May.

When time permits, Deedra and I visit back and forth. Deedra Cox Thompson is president/owner of a successful licensed pet sitting business in West Palm Beach, Florida, named **"Pet at Home"**.

Everyone seems to love animals....I hope that perhaps this book will make you smile and remember a time when you interacted with one of God's creatures and knew that you had somehow shared an extraordinary experience that you would never forget. Maybe that experience was at a zoo....and maybe it was at Coxville Zoo on a Sunday afternoon. Perhaps, your own childhood photo album contains a picture of you as you rode one of the ponies. If it does then chances are your parents took your picture to preserve the memory of your smiles and laughter that day!

Dedicated to our "one and only" Grandson:
Christopher Michael Robinson

"Wind Beneath Our Wings"

My father, Alvin Cox, passed away from natural
causes at the age of 79, on April 28, 1996.
There is an old expression that implies that when
someone was made, the pattern was thrown away.
This best describes my dad, as he was truly unique.
The legacy he left is one of kindness, gentleness,
love, and understanding of all of God's creatures.
He truly was the
"Wind Beneath Our Wings".

The picture on the back cover of this book was taken by
William E. Lummus. It appeared in the Austin American Statesman
along with Bill Brammer's article on April 15, 1954. The caption
underneath the picture read as follow: "Neighborliness – All the
habitués of Coxville Zoo get along fine with each other. There may
be a few recalcitrants in their midst, but the dog and monkey
certainly typifies the friendship and flower scheme on the Dallas
Highway. They are just one big happy, furry, fuzzy family."

1632018

Made in the USA